GW00402169

PC tune-up
Handbook

Unleash your PC's potential and keep it in tip-top working order

Paul Wardley

An imprint of **Pearson Education**

London · Boston · Indianapolis · New York · Mexico City ·
Toronto · Sydney · Tokyo · Singapore · Hong Kong · Cape Town
New Delhi · Madrid · Paris · Amsterdam · Munich · Milan · Stockholm

PEARSON EDUCATION LIMITED

Head Office
Edinburgh Gate
Harlow CM20 2JE
Tel: +44 (0)1279 623623
Fax: +44 (0)1279 431059

London Office:
128 Long Acre
London WC2E 9AN
Tel: +44 (0)20 7447 2000
Fax: +44 (0)20 7240 5771
Website:*www.it-minds.com*

First published in Great Britain in 2002 by Pearson Education

© VNU Business Publications, 2001

VNU House, 32–34 Broadwick Street, London W1A 2HG

ISBN 0-130-64824-8

The right of Paul Wardley to be identified as author of
this work has been asserted by him.

Edited by Mick Andon
Designed by slowcat (info@slowcat.com)
Illustrations by Spike Gerrell
Typeset by Pantek Arts Ltd, Maidstone, Kent
Printed and bound by Rotolito Lombarda, Italy

The publishers' policy is to use paper manufactured from sustainable forests.

Contents

About the author

Paul Wardley, paul_wardley@hotmail.com, served his time as a programmer, college lecturer, computer systems administrator and technical editor of *What PC?* Having been released for good behaviour, he now develops training resources, writes for several computer magazines, is a regular contributor to Computer*active*, and works as a consultant specialising in training and education. It is his ambition to find time to build his own website.

Acknowledgements

We are grateful to the following for permission to reproduce copyright material:

AMN Software; Creative Labs, Inc.; Dacris Software; En Tech Taiwan; Fuji Xerox Australia; MadOnion.com Oy; Perfex Ltd.; radsoft.net; SiSoftware (UK); Tiny Computers Ltd.; www.fi.muni.cz.

Screenshots on pages 18 and 22 reprinted with permission from ViewSonic Corporation, USA; Screenshots on pages 52 and 66 reprinted with permission from PowerQuest Corporation, PowerQuest and Drive Image are trademarks or registered trademarks of PowerQuest Corporation in the USA and/or elsewhere; Screenshot on page 54 reprinted with permission from CNET, Inc. © Copyright 1995–2001, www.cnet.com; Screenshot on page 57 © Research Machines plc, 2000, used with the kind permission of Research Machines plc.; Screenshots on pages 67 and 78 reprinted by permission from Symantec Corporation; Microsoft screenshots and box shots reprinted by permission from Microsoft Corporation; WinZip screen images reproduced with permission of WinZip Computing, Inc. Copyright 1991–2001 WinZip Computing, Inc. WinZip® is a registered trademark of WinZip Computing, Inc. WinZip is available from www.winzip.com.

In some instances we have been unable to trace the owners of copyright material, and we would appreciate any information that would enable us to do so.

INTRODUCTION Getting started

Welcome to the third book in the Computer*active* StepbyStep series. If you've read any of the others, you'll know what to expect: a direct approach that leads you through everything you need to know about tuning your PC, with lots of examples and a step-by-step workshop at the end of each chapter.

As before, we avoid jargon wherever we can (anything you do need to know is explained in the jargon busters at the end), and we've arranged things so that if you work through the book chapter by chapter, you can be sure of doing the right things in the right order. You don't need to bring any special skills or experience with you, apart from being able to work comfortably with Windows®.

While we don't promise to turn your PC into the fastest piece of silicon this side of

Seattle, we can help you get it back to the reliable state it should have been in when you bought it, and with a little luck we can show you how to make a few tweaks here and there that will make your PC run even faster than it did when new.

How the book is arranged

To make it easier for you to find things when looking back on what you've read, each of the eight chapters begins with a brief summary of what's covered within. The first six have been designed for 'hands-on' reading, while the last two are mainly for reference, but you'll get more out of the book if you skim through the whole thing at one sitting and then come back to it for a practical session after arming yourself with a few software tools.

Introduction: what you'll need

We've made every effort to make this book as useful as possible to people who have no software other than Windows, and instead of telling you to go out and buy commercial programs that check out your PC, fix damaged files and tune up your hard disk, we explain how to do these things yourself using only the utility programs built into Windows. Chapter 8 contains an alphabetical run through all of these, with a brief explanation of what each one does and which version of Windows you'll find it in.

Where there is no Windows software tool for a particular job – speeding up a graphics card by 'overclocking' it, for example – we've turned to programs that can be downloaded freely from the world wide web, but we've kept these to a minimum for the sake of people who don't have their own connection to the internet. Even if your interests lie away from the internet and you're not already a regular user, we recommend setting up a trial subscription for the purpose of downloading the updates and enhancements mentioned in this book. There are plenty of service providers offering free accounts with no hidden charges. All you pay are the local call charges for the time you spend connected, which, if you stick to evening and weekend rates, shouldn't break the bank.

Which Windows?

The Windows you are using is likely to be Windows 98, though there are still some older machines running Windows 95 and plenty of PCs bought since late 2000 that are pre-installed with Windows Me. Almost everything in this book will work with any of these three versions of Windows, which are collectively known as Windows 9x, the main exceptions being Drive Converter (Windows 98 only) and System Restore (only in Windows Me).

What this book does not cover is Windows XP, which is the very latest version of Windows. Despite offering many of the familiar features of Windows 9x, this is completely different under the skin.

To be sure of getting the latest version of a downloadable program, your best plan is to visit the website of its supplier, but sites such as www.vnunet.com are useful one-stop shops for popular utility and tune-up programs.

Windows XP might look like nothing more than a designer version of its predecessors, but below the surface there have been major changes that make many of the procedures described in this book unsuitable for it.

Introduction: benchmarking

Tuning a PC is not a branch of nuclear physics. In fact it's no more complicated than spring cleaning – you fix things and clean things, throw away junk, and replace faulty items with new ones. Each step that you take has only a marginal impact on overall performance, but cumulatively you end up with significant improvements.

Gains can be made in two areas: reliability and performance. Reliability is not something you measure: you simply enjoy the absence of unexplained crashes and hang-ups that might otherwise have caused you to lose work. Performance testing is another matter because there are ways of objectively measuring the speed of a PC using benchmarking software.

Component- and system-level tests

There is no built-in Windows software to measure performance. The nearest thing is a program called System Monitor, which shows the activity of some of the internal workings of your PC in real time using constantly updated graphs, but System Monitor doesn't actually produce a figure you can use as a yardstick to measure speed improvements. For this you'll need to download a benchmarking program from the web.

There are two approaches to benchmarking. The most common method is to measure the speed of individual components such as the hard disk or graphics card by counting the number of bytes transferred or frames displayed per second. The other method is more complicated but gives more meaningful results. It's called application benchmarking and works by measuring the time taken to run a series of tasks that are typical of those a PC has to perform while running ordinary programs.

Whichever type you use, it really doesn't matter how well your PC measures up to some hypothetical standard suggested by the program. What's important is that you

know your PC's score before tuning so that you can compare it with the results afterwards. Your choice of benchmarking program isn't crucial, but you must use the same one before and after tuning, and you must run it under the same conditions. Ideally, you'd test immediately after starting your PC and with no other programs running, always using the same display settings for screen size and number of colours.

The Dacris benchmarks (from www.dacris.com) and the Dr Hardware benchmarks (from www.dr-hardware.com) are component-level test programs. The Dacris benchmarks are very easy to use but you can only run them ten times unless you pay for them. The Dr Hardware tests can be run as often as you like.

For benchmarking 3D graphics, you can download 3DMark 2001 (the program Computeractive testers use) from www.madonion.com. The snag is that it's 40Mb in size. An easier alternative is to check whether any of the games you own has a test mode built into it. Many of them do.

3

Introduction: On your marks

As well as making a note of the pre-tuning benchmark results, it's worth recording the size of the hard disk (or disks) in your PC, and how much space is used and free on each of them. With these tasks out of the way, there's just one crucial thing left to do, which is to make a backup.

The right sort of backup

A data backup isn't good enough; you need a complete backup of everything on your Windows hard disk – and you must know how to reinstate the backup from MS-DOS®. Imagine that everything has been removed from your hard disk, including Windows. That's the situation you need to be able to recover from. If you think you don't know what MS-DOS is, you're wrong; it's the mainly blank text screen you get when you boot from a Windows Startup floppy disk.

If you've never developed the habit of making backups, perhaps because you

thought you had nothing worth backing up, skip now to page 65, where the various techniques are described. Of course, you'll need something to store the backup on, which means a Zip drive or some other form of high-capacity recording device – perhaps a tape drive or CD-RW drive. You could also use a second hard disk, either one inside your PC or one plugged into the back, or even another PC that's connected to yours on a network.

If none of these backup options are available and you can't borrow a backup drive, you'll be treading on very thin ice when you try some of the techniques in this book. We can't stop you tuning your PC without a backup, but don't say we didn't warn you.

Hardware problems?

This is a book about tuning PCs, not repairing them, so we've made the assumption that your PC is up and running, even if it isn't running as well as you'd like it to. If you've bought this book hoping to breathe life into a dead or dying PC, all we can offer you is Chapter 7, in which you'll find information on troubleshooting a selection of worrying (but usually non-fatal) errors.

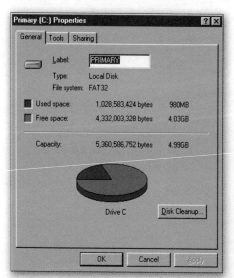

To determine the size of your Windows hard disk and how much of it is already in use, double-click the My Computer icon on the Windows Desktop, then right-click drive C: and select Properties. If you have any other hard disks, check the space remaining on these too.

The notion that a backup is meant only to protect valuable corporate data is outmoded. The average user stores few or no critical data, but a full system backup enables Windows and a full set of inter-related programs to be recovered in minutes instead of days.

4

CHAPTER 1 Your PC inside out

What's in this chapter?

You can't tune a PC unless you have some idea of what goes on inside the system box and how all the hardware elements interact with the Windows operating system. Fortunately, you don't need to be a computer expert to tune a PC, just as you don't need to be a house builder if all you want to do is decorate one. In this chapter, we tell you all you need to know before starting tuning, and what you need to do in advance.

Disk discovery

As we take you on a quick tour of your PC, you'll probably realise you already know more about it than you think. You're sure to be aware there's a hard disk spinning away madly inside it because you can hear it

thrashing away whenever you switch on the PC and every time you load a program. You may already know that the hard disk stores all the programs on your PC, along with all the files (pictures, documents, video and music) that you create, but don't forget it's also home to Windows, and because the hard disk is bound up so intimately with the software and the operating system, it's a prime target for tuning and tweaking.

Incidentally, the hard disk is virtually silent when it's just ticking over, so the constant whirring sound you hear from the bowels of the system unit is far more likely to come from its cooling fans. There's one in the power supply, another on the processor, and sometimes an extra one on the graphics card or bolted to the front panel.

Your PC: a lightning tour

The central processor

Central processing unit is a bit of a mouthful so most people say 'CPU'. It's the part of your PC that does all the 'thinking'. Sometimes it's characterised as the brain of a PC, sometimes the heart or the motor. It doesn't matter how you think of it; what's important from the tuner's point of view is that you can't do anything to speed it up or improve its performance – at least not officially. The CPU is there when you buy your PC and if it's not fast enough you're supposed to throw it away and plug in a more powerful one.

Unofficially, as you'll see in Chapter 5, you can speed up a CPU by running it hotter than its makers intended. Yes, we tell you how to do it, but we don't actually recommend it. Think of it as a resuscitation technique for a machine that's already on its last legs, not as something to be tried as a matter of course. There are plenty of tried and tested tuning techniques you can use in complete safety.

Memory

Acronyms abound in the world of computing, and hot on the heels of CPU comes another one: RAM. Don't worry, we'll only be using acronyms when they help to avoid confusion. RAM, as you probably know, is memory, and you might also know that the initials stand for Random Access Memory, even if you're not quite sure what the memory remembers.

The truth is that RAM doesn't remember anything. Every time you switch off a PC, the RAM is wiped clean, as completely and irrevocably as names scrawled in the sand are wiped out by the tide. The difference is that memory is wiped instantly, so if you really want a computer to remember something you store it on the hard disk, not in RAM.

It would be unfair to tell you that RAM can't remember anything without telling you

what it's really for, which is workspace. It's where the processor and the hard disk store things temporarily until they need them.

CPUs come in all shapes and sizes, but there are just two major suppliers, Intel and AMD. Most companies would prefer you to buy a new processor than try to tweak the one you've got.

System memory comes on plug-in modules that are cheap to buy and easy to fit. Tuning can help make the most of your existing memory, but if you haven't got enough of it the only option is to buy more.

Your PC: a lightning tour (continued)

Having plenty of workspace really speeds up a PC. Imagine you're handed a thousand different business cards and asked to put them in alphabetical order. Just as you're about to start sorting them into 26 piles, one for each letter of the alphabet, you're told that you can't put them down and you have to keep them in your hands. You can still sort them, of course, but only with a lot of fumbling and shuffling, and the job is likely to take you ten times as long as it would if you could lay them out on a table.

To a computer, RAM is the work surface. It's a space where thousands or even millions of items of information can be juggled while the CPU deals with them. Clearly, the best way of increasing the amount of workspace is to add more RAM, though in Chapter 3 we show you how to make the best use of whatever memory there is in your PC.

Though we've talked about RAM as if it were all in one place, it's not. The main block of memory is system RAM – and this is what's referred to in advertisements when you see figures of 32Mb, 64Mb or more – but just about every component in a PC has its own supply of RAM for private use.

Graphics and expansion cards

The graphics card is the second biggest store of RAM in most PCs. On recent cards, 16Mb is typical, but 32Mb and even 64Mb are not uncommon in machines designed for playing fast-action games. The graphics card is more properly (and more accurately) called the display adapter, but we'll stick to graphics card because it's the term that most people understand.

A card, by the way, is any device you can push into one of the internal expansion slots of a PC. It takes the form of a printed circuit board with components soldered onto it. Along one edge is a row of contacts that lines up with a similar set inside the expansion slot.

The cheapest place to buy RAM is from a specialist web supplier. Prices change from day to day and competition is fierce, so be sure to compare prices and check availability before you order. At www.crucial.com there is plenty of guidance on choosing the right type of memory for your particular machine.

High-performance graphics cards with their own processors are a good buy. They not only provide faster graphics but also take some of the strain off the main CPU, leaving it with more resources to spare for Windows.

Your PC: a lightning tour (continued)

Expansion cards need to be physically connected to the main circuit board (motherboard) of a PC in order to draw electrical power and communicate with the CPU. The system of contacts along one edge of a circuit is very convenient. No soldering is required and any component can be upgraded simply by plugging in a new one.

In a traditionally constructed PC, three of the expansion slots are occupied by the graphics card, sound card and modem, the others being for your own add-ons. In some budget PCs, there may be no expansion cards at all, the same functions being carried out by chips soldered permanently to the motherboard. Though these integrated machines are cheaper to produce, they pose more problems when it comes to upgrading. For the purposes of tuning, it doesn't matter whether devices are supplied on cards or built into the motherboard.

Peripheral vision

All the components mentioned so far (hard disk, CPU, RAM and expansion cards) are housed inside the main case or system unit of the computer. Also in here are the power supply and more drives – almost certainly a floppy disk drive and probably one or more optical drives for CDs and DVDs.

The rest of a computer system consists of peripheral devices, and the only thing these have in common is that is that they're not inside the system unit. The range is staggering. It includes keyboards, mice, joysticks, digital cameras, scanners, games pads, monitors, printers, camcorders, global positioning systems, editing decks, musical instruments – the list is as long as your pockets are deep.

To anybody interested in tuning PCs, the significance of peripherals is the way they connect to the computer and the drain they make on the rest of the system. Despite their own knobs and buttons, all peripherals ultimately fall under the control of Windows,

which means we have a chance to influence the way they operate and perhaps coax a little more out of them, or at least minimise the negative impact they might have on overall system performance.

To change a motherboard, you have to dismantle and virtually rebuild your PC. If you fill all the expansion slots, you can save yourself the trouble of fitting a new motherboard by buying Universal Serial Bus (USB) accessories that plug into sockets on the back of the computer.

Your PC won't look exactly like this one but it will certainly contain similar devices and components.

Identifying components

Knowing what's inside a PC might be enough to impress your friends and help you hold up your end of a conversation about buying a computer, but it's not enough if you want to try your hand at tuning. For this, you need hard facts about individual components: makes, model numbers and specifications. You don't need any technical knowledge of how these components work but you do need to know their characteristics – such as the capacity of hard disk, the speed of a modem, or the amount of memory on a graphics card.

Finding out these details isn't always as easy as you'd think. This is because PCs are assembled using components sourced from a number of different suppliers. No manufacturer makes every component from scratch, so finding out exactly what's inside your PC can be quite tricky.

The name and model number of a PC can act as a guide to what it contains – a Speedo P3-700 is almost certainly based on a 700MHz Pentium III processor – but this doesn't tell you about the rest of the system. Even if you have a manual for your machine, it may not be accurate because manufacturers frequently change individual components when technically superior or cheaper alternatives become available.

The best guide to what's inside a PC is the packing list that should have accompanied it. This list is the one used during assembly and it specifies every component used to build the machine plus all the software and accessories bundled with it.

Device Manager

If you don't have a packing list or system specification, you'll have to do a bit of detective work. There's a handy Windows program called Device Manager that you can use to make a list of the main components of your PC and how they're being used by Windows. This is doubly useful

because if you accidentally change a setting when tuning your PC, you can put things right by referring to the printed Device Manager report. Find out how to make one of these on the next page, and be sure to keep a copy in a safe place.

Technical specifications Thunderbird 900	
Case:	ATX Midi Tower
Processor:	AMD Thunderbird 900 MHz CPU
Motherboard:	Asus A7V, ATX format
RAM:	128 MB SDRAM
HDD:	30 GB Maxtor
FDD:	3.5", 1.44 MB
CD ROM:	8xHitachi DVD Drive
Graphics:	GeForce 2 GTS, 32 MB AGP
Sound:	SB Live 1024 + Microphone
Modem:	56K Internal V90 voice fax/modem, hardware
Network card	Optional
Keyboard:	Microsoft Win 9x UK Keyboard PS2
Mouse:	Microsoft Intellimouse with scroll wheel PS2
Speakers:	FPS 1000 self powered stereo speakers
Monitor:	17" Iiyama Visionmaster A705MT Diamondtr
Software:	Windows 98SE, Lotus Samrt Suite Millenniur Cillin Anti-Virus + programs that ship as stan soundcard, the Creative graphics card and th
Others:	2 x serial, 1 x parallel, 2 x USB
Warranty:	12 months parts and labour RTB + 4 years labour RTB + free upgrading (se
Price:	£999 + vat (See notes)

Most people throw away the packing list or specification sheet that accompanies their PC when they dispose of its packaging, but a list of the components inside a machine is invaluable when it comes to tuning a PC or requesting technical support.

SiSoft Sandra 2001 is a downloadable tuning tool that can help you determine what's inside your PC. It's free to private users at www.sisoftware.co.uk/Sandra

There's a host of third-party commercial and shareware programs designed to help you identify and test PC hardware. The resource summary produced by Device Manager is concerned not so much with identifying the components as with how Windows uses them. If you have a third-party program such as Norton SystemWorks or SiSoft Sandra, use it, but don't neglect to print a Device Manager resource summary too. This will be useful if, when you're tuning your PC, you want to restore any of the original settings.

1 Start Device Manager from the Windows Desktop by right-clicking on My Computer and selecting Properties from the drop-down shortcut menu. This opens the System Properties box. On the General tab, you can see which version of Windows you're using, how much system RAM it has, and what sort of processor is fitted.

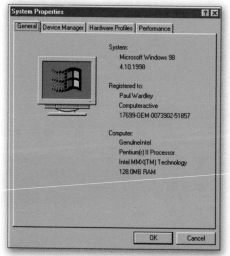

2 Select the Device Manager tab to display a list of the components inside your machine. As shown here, instead of makes and models all you see are broad categories such as Disk drives and Display adapters, but a printed resource summary includes a wealth of extra detail.

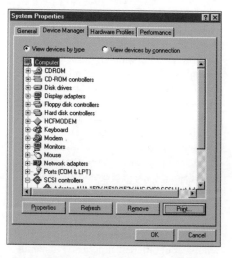

3 Click the Print button and you're offered three types of report. Unless you've previously selected a component in Device Manager, the middle option (Selected class or device) will be greyed out and unavailable. This doesn't matter because the option you need is the first one, System summary. For the average PC, this will print on just three pages of A4 paper, whereas the third option (All devices and system summary) produces so much detail you could end up with 20 pages of facts and figures. Select System summary and click OK.

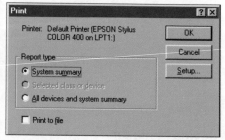

Device Manager has its limitations and can't tell you everything you need to know about your PC's hardware. It can't, for example, tell you the exact make and model of your hard disk, but it does tell you its general type, how much data it can store, and how it has been formatted – which for tuning purposes is all you need.

Understanding resources

The printout of the resource summary has seven sections. Some of the information looks rather intimidating, but it's easy to follow once you know what to look for. The first section is a system overview. Amongst other things, this tells you the version of Windows you're running, the type of processor inside your PC, and details of the motherboard's basic input/output system (BIOS).

If the Windows version number at the start of the report is 4.00.950 or 4.00.950A, you have the original release of Windows 95, but there were several revised and improved versions of Windows 95 (collectively referred to as OSR2) with the following version numbers:
4.00.1111, 4.03.1212, 4.03.1213, 4.03.1214, 4.00.950B. 4.00.950C
Windows 98 (version 4.10.1998) was introduced in November 1998 and revamped the following year as Windows 98 Second Edition (version 4.10.2222A). You don't really need to be told whether you have Windows Me, but for completeness the version number is 4.90.3000.

The later the version, the more features it offers. Support for USB accessories was added right at the end of Windows 95's career but was standard in Windows 98, as was a more efficient disk-filing system. In Windows 98 Second Edition, there were the inevitable bug fixes, better support for the latest hardware devices, and enhanced internet features. Windows Me was the showcase for a number of ease-of-use, security and multimedia enhancements that have since been incorporated in Windows XP.

BIOS basics
Three lines of the summary refer to the computer's BIOS (Basic Input/Output System). This is a programmable chip whose contents can be updated by downloading new code from the web. The updating technique is called 'flashing'. This is not something seedy

that could land you behind bars, but it is a risky process that can leave your PC incapacitated if there's a power failure part-way through. For this reason, we don't recommend flash upgrading a BIOS unless you've bought an upgrade processor and the old BIOS won't work with it. If you have a Pentium III CPU and it is reported as a Pentium II, don't worry: this is a common glitch and doesn't mean you've got a duff processor or need a BIOS upgrade.

If your copy of Windows came in a box or on a CD-ROM, you don't really need a version number to tell you which one you're using, but you do if your only copy of Windows is an image on a hard disk.

If you suspect that Windows is not identifying your CPU correctly, download TestCPU from www.fi.muni.cz/~xsmid4. It's foolproof and it's free.

11

Understanding resources (continued)

Interrupts

The IRQ summary is a list of interrupt requests. These are 16 odd-sounding beasts, numbered from 00 to 15. Think of them as phone lines that connect devices such as sound cards, keyboards and modems to the CPU. When a device needs to interrupt the CPU and ask it to do something, it uses its designated line so the CPU knows which device it is talking to. Some devices can share a single interrupt, others can't. You need to know how the interrupts have been dealt out in case of conflicts.

Ports and more

The summaries of I/O port and upper memory usage look bewildering, but they're straightforward lists showing blocks of memory that have been reserved for use by individual components. The line below is typical.

0200h-0207h – Gameport joystick

All it says is that 8 bytes of memory numbered from 0200 to 0207 have been reserved for use by the joystick. The 'h' after the numbers stands for hexadecimal, which is a convenient way of counting for computers. Some hexadecimal numbers look very odd indeed because they contain the letters A to F, representing the decimal numbers 10–15, but they're just numbers and you don't have to learn how they work. Their significance to people tuning Windows is that they identify blocks of memory, and if two devices use the same block, one of the devices won't work properly.

The direct memory access (DMA) summary has much in common with the IRQ summary. Any device that is able to delve straight into memory instead of doing things the official way by going through the CPU needs one of the DMA channels. These are allocated by Windows during the boot sequence, but in case of conflicts you need to know which device is using which channel. The DMA usage summary tells you. The last two sections of the resource summary report confirm how much memory is in your PC and the capacity and partitioning of the disk drives. Partitioning is a neat trick that's explained in the workshop on page 50.

If you want to view a summary of interrupt requests but you don't need a printed report, highlight Computer at the top of the Device Manager list and click the Properties button.

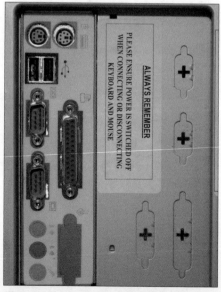

The term 'port' is one of those odd bits of computer jargon (like interface) that carries an extra shade of meaning to those in the know. This picture shows the physical port connectors for external accessories.

Tuning made simple

Configure Windows Explorer

While tuning, you'll need to hunt down, examine and possibly replace individual files. This is done most easily with Windows Explorer, though you can open folders on the Windows Desktop if you prefer. Whatever method you choose, you need to set up a more structured display of information than Windows displays by default.

Start Windows Explorer and click on the Windows folder. On a freshly installed Windows system, a warning appears on the right that modifying the contents of the system folder may cause programs to stop working correctly. If this happens to you, get rid of the message by opening the View menu and clicking Details.

● On the View menu, click Folder options to open a dialogue box. In this box, select the View tab. In the list of Advanced settings, tick the following boxes:
– Display the full path in title bar.
– Show all files (this is in the Hidden files section).
● Untick the box next to Hide file extensions for known file types.
● After making these selections, you can ensure that every folder is governed by the same settings. Click the Like Current Folder button. Click Yes to confirm. Click OK.

Get hold of a zip manager

At some stage when tuning, you'll need to work with zipped files. These are ordinary files that have been compressed to save space. Before you can use them, they have to be unzipped to expand them to their original size. Windows Me can manage this using its system of compressed folders, but for Windows 95 and Windows 98 you'll need a third-party utility.

Check the selection at www.vnunet.com. There are several that are suitable in the Downloads section under Utilities – File Management – Compression. WinZip is a popular choice if all you want is file compression, but if you'd like a zip tool

that's also a better file manager than Windows Explorer, go for OnTrack's PowerDesk 4. Whatever program you decide on, experiment with it using junk files before you start tuning your PC.

Without making these simple changes to Windows Explorer, you won't be able to tune your PC effectively.

WinZip is a powerful tool, but unless you're familiar with compressed files it's not immediately obvious how to use it. Fortunately there's a wizard to guide you through the three most common tasks.

One of the things that gives PowerDesk 4 the edge over Windows Explorer is that you can work simultaneously with two disks or folders, each displayed in its own panel. You don't have to start a second copy of the program.

Before you can tune your PC for performance and reliability, you need to make sure it's in some semblance of working order. This workshop helps you resolve existing hardware conflicts caused by two pieces of equipment fighting over the same resources. You may need to come back to this workshop later if a conflict develops after you've updated any of the supporting software for your hardware.

1 If one device is in conflict with another, it's highlighted in Device Manager by a yellow exclamation mark. If a device is disabled or not working at all, it is marked with a red cross. Check your hardware now by right-clicking My Computer, selecting Properties from the drop-down shortcut menu, and clicking the Device Manager tab. Look for the telltale signs of exclamation signs and crosses. If there are no conflicts, the list will look like the one on page 10.

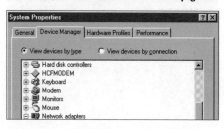

2 In this example, the sound card has been disabled and is marked by a red cross. To enable any device that has been disabled, double-click the Device Manager entry for the component. This

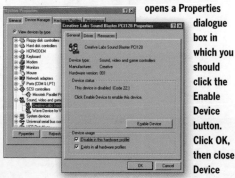

opens a Properties dialogue box in which you should click the Enable Device button. Click OK, then close Device

Manager. It's a good idea to reboot after enabling a device, regardless of whether you're told to. If after enabling a device it still doesn't work, look for a conflict with another device.

3 To resolve a conflict between two devices (one of them will be highlighted by a yellow exclamation mark), start by double-clicking the marked device, then click its Resources tab. Note whether the conflict is in the Input/Output Range or the Interrupt Request. In this case, it's an I/O range conflict.

4 Remove the tick from the box next to Use automatic settings. Click on the Input/Output range that is causing the problem, and then click the Change Settings button. You may now select another, non-

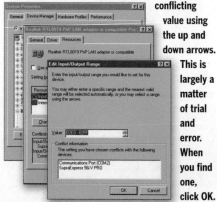

conflicting value using the up and down arrows. This is largely a matter of trial and error. When you find one, click OK.

5 The conflict has apparently been resolved but will the new setting work? Click OK again and you'll be warned that your manual settings will prevent Windows from changing the I/O range in the future. Click Yes to confirm that you want to continue. Windows will now try to implement the new settings and you may be asked to insert the Windows CD-ROM. All being well, the conflict is now resolved. Reboot your PC and check.

6 If the conflict is over interrupt requests rather than I/O ranges, it can be solved in a similar way, but you may find that there are no free interrupts. In this case, you need to find one that has been allocated but isn't being used. The obvious

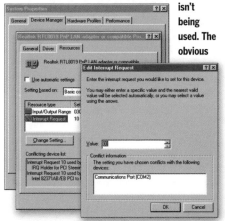

candidates are the serial ports on the back of your PC. Find one that has nothing plugged into it and assign its interrupt to the problem device. You should also disable the serial port using your computer's BIOS Setup program, as described on page 35.

7 If you can't find an I/O range or interrupt that will make a problem device work, or Windows tells you that the device cannot be modified (as shown

above), try attacking the problem from another angle – that of the conflicting device. It may be that the other device can use a different set of ranges or interrupts. It's at times like this that you'll be glad you printed out the Device Manager resource report. It's easy to lose track of where you started from once you get involved in the trial and error resolution of conflicts.

8 If you apparently resolve a conflict but the device still doesn't work, check its documentation. Some older expansion cards are not designed for Plug and Play operation (network and SCSI cards are the usual culprits). They may have switches or jumpers on the card that have to be adjusted manually in order to use a different I/O range or interrupt. Change the settings on the card to agree with those that are set in Device Manager.

CHAPTER 2

Sorting out your driver

What's in this chapter?

This chapter tells you what drivers are and identifies the components in your PC that need them. You'll find out how to track down the existing drivers in your system and work out whether they're old or new, and how to compare them with those available on the internet. If the existing ones are past their sell-by dates, you can download replacements. The workshop at the end of this chapter steps you through the various means of installing them.

Why drivers are important

A Windows PC is a tightly-knit collection of components from different manufacturers. These components or devices have to communicate with each other and with Windows. The physical links between components are through cables and circuits on the motherboard, but the link to Windows is handled by something called a driver or, to give it its full name, a device driver.

A device driver is a very clever invention that allows Microsoft to keep Windows up to date and manufacturers to introduce new hardware devices independently. Suppose that one of the leading graphics card manufacturers produces a new model that is not recognised by any of the existing versions of Windows. If Windows were an inflexible operating system, the company would not be able to sell the card until it had persuaded Microsoft to rewrite Windows to support it, and even then they'd only be able to sell it to people with the new version of Windows.

The elegant solution to the problem of constantly evolving hardware and software is the driver. This is a small, renewable segment of program that handles the communication between a hardware component and Windows. As long as the driver tells Windows what's going on, Windows doesn't care how the component is doing it. A great many drivers are built into Windows – covering most of the popular hardware devices from major manufacturers. If a vendor develops a new piece of equipment or makes changes and improvements to an existing item, a new driver is supplied to replace the one built into Windows.

Original drivers

Drivers used to be supplied on floppy disks but these days they're always on CD-ROM. When you buy a ready-to-run PC, the computer manufacturer pre-installs Windows and all the essential drivers, but you still need copies of the drivers in case they ever need to be reinstated. These may be provided on a handful of CD-ROMs, but sometimes the computer manufacturer compiles them onto a single CD for your convenience, and if you're really lucky there'll be a menu and help system to help you install them.

If your PC apparently came without drivers, it could be that they are installed in a folder on the hard disk of your PC. This is a cheap option for the supplier and it's convenient for you – it's impossible to lose your driver disks under a pile of papers, for example – but it can lead to problems if you ever have to reformat or replace the hard disk. In this case, you will lose all the drivers unless you first copy them onto some kind of backup drive.

Unfortunately, drivers have something in common with socks. They have the habit of disappearing whenever they are moved. With socks, it's on the journey from the laundry basket to the washing machine, but with drivers, it's whenever a PC moves from one owner to another. By the time a PC reaches its third owner, it has usually lost every driver disk or CD it ever possessed.

These days drivers come on CD-ROMs rather than floppy disks.

Restore Pack

Windows 98 Restore

This CD contains an "Image" of a default install of Windows 98. If you insert the supplied floppy disk and re-boot your computer it will set the contents of the hard disk back to a basic working version.

WARNING: This is only to be used in a disaster situation as it will remove all data and applications that you have installed.

> Video Live Mail
> Power VCR
> Tiny Online (UK)
> TextBridge Classic 2.0 OCR
> Microsoft DirectX 7.0
> Microsoft DirectX Media

Description
Application for TV recording software

[Install]   [Help]   [Exit]

Suppliers of home PCs often provide a system recovery CD that can restore a damaged Windows system to its factory-fresh condition. In doing so, it overwrites everything already stored on the hard disk, so you have to be careful not to confuse a recovery CD with one that merely holds drivers.

Customising your Desktop step by step

Lost drivers

Losing a set of original drivers is not as disastrous as it sounds. New ones are available free of charge from the websites of component manufacturers. You don't have to be the original purchaser of the hardware in question (receipts and serial numbers are not demanded), and because drivers are usually quite short programs they don't cost a fortune to download.

The only snag in getting hold of drivers is when you don't have an internet account or when your computer is out of commission. It shouldn't be too hard to arrange to download drivers at work or from a friend's machine (though to keep the friendship alive, you should pay for the cost of the call), and failing this you can buy an hour's web access at an internet cafe, local IT training centre or public library. It used to be possible to request drivers by phone and receive them through the post, but such is the way of the wired world that nowadays it's almost impossible to get this kind of service.

Improved drivers

It's not only drivers you've lost that need to be replaced. Ensuring that all your hardware drivers are up to date is an essential part of tuning your PC. Hardware manufacturers frequently revamp their drivers to correct bugs in the originals and to make improvements, so switching to the most recent drivers might make your PC faster and add to its capabilities. At the very least, you know you are running with the drivers most likely to work reliably with the rest of the system.

As to how often you should check for new drivers, it depends whether you're experiencing problems with the old ones. If not, a quick check every six months should be fine, but don't leave it longer than a year and always update drivers as a preliminary to tuning your PC. To make it easier to keep you informed of the availability of updated

drivers, some suppliers ask you to supply an email address when you download new drivers, with the promise of contacting you when replacements become available.

Most download sites tell you the size of the file before you start downloading. If you use a standard 56K modem and an ordinary telephone line, expect to download 250–350Kb per minute.

If you're asked for an email address when downloading drivers, you can give a false one. This avoids the danger of junk mail but also means the supplier won't be able to let you know when new drivers become available. It's your choice.

With an out-of-date driver any piece of equipment is likely to function 'less than optimally' (to use manufacturers' language). Even when a component seems to be working perfectly, it's worth checking regularly for new drivers because these may improve performance. Having the most up-to-date drivers for a printer, scanner or backup device might not seem crucially important, but there are four key components whose drivers have such an impact on performance that you should never set about tuning a PC until you've checked or renewed them:

- Graphics card
- Sound card
- Modem
- Monitor.

Know your hardware

To be sure of getting the right drivers for a component, you need to know at least its make and name, but more often than not you also need a precise model number. Armed with these, you won't waste time vaguely looking for drivers for a Diamond SupraExpress modem (which is a bit like looking for a Ford Mondeo in a company car park when you don't know the colour or the registration). Instead you'll be able to home in specifically on a Diamond SupraExpress 56i V Pro.

If you printed out the resource report described in the previous chapter, you're already half way to identifying the hardware in your PC. Simply look down the list of interrupts or I/O ranges until you find the item you're looking for. If the description is insufficient to identify the exact make and model – and you haven't got a packing list or specification sheet – you'll need to glean the facts from elsewhere, perhaps by opening up the machine and looking inside.

Another source of information is the messages that flash up on the screen when you start your computer. On some machines these are suppressed, but on most PCs the make and model of the graphics card flashes up first. Immediately after this (you can freeze the display if you hit the Pause key quickly enough) come serial numbers for the motherboard and BIOS, and you might even catch models and serial numbers for the CPU and CD-ROM drives.

The only way to be certain what's inside your PC is to take a look. Most hardware items are plastered with information and serial numbers, but you might need a torch and a screwdriver to find them.

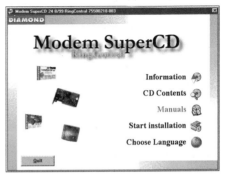

If drivers are supplied on a CD-ROM, it's worth looking to see if there's online documentation too. In the absence of a CD menu, use Windows Explorer to browse for folders called Manuals or Docs.

Dating your drivers

Before logging on to the web and searching for new drivers, make a list of the ones you already have and how old they are. For each driver, you need to discover its file version and date. There are several places in Windows where you can track down this information, but the first port of call is, of course, Device Manager.

By the way, if you've been starting Device Manager by going into System Properties from the Windows Desktop and then right-clicking on My Computer and selecting Properties, it's about time you learnt the quick way. Hold down one of the Windows (flag symbol) keys and tap Pause. This jumps straight to System Properties without you having to make a detour via the Windows Desktop.

1 With the System Properties box on the screen, click the Device Manager tab to start tracking down your existing drivers. You should see a long alphabetical list with CD-ROM near the start and, if you scroll down, USB ports at the end. If yours is a much shorter list starting with Advanced Power Management, click View devices by type instead of View devices by connection. These two choices are just below the tabs at the top of the dialogue box.

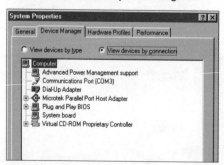

2 From here, you work on one device at a time. Taking the graphics card as an example, you identify its driver by double-clicking on Display adapters, then double-clicking the name of the graphics card. This displays a Properties dialogue box that has a

Driver tab. Click this and you'll be able to read the provider of the driver (Microsoft, Matrox, Creative or whatever) and a date. Note that dates are displayed in the US style of month-day-year.

3 At the bottom of the Driver tab are two buttons: one to update the driver and another labelled Driver File details. Click the latter and you'll be presented with a supplementary dialogue box. Look here for three lines labelled Provider, File version and Copyright. Make a note of the file version. Use similar techniques to identify the remaining drivers on your list.

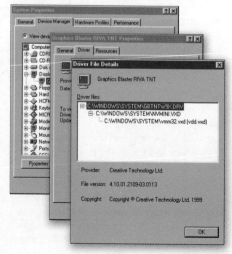

More driver information

Printer drivers

Printer drivers seldom show any useful details in Device Manager, but they do in System Information. You'll find this by clicking the Start button and selecting Programs, then Accessories, then System Tools. Click System Information to start the program. In the left-hand panel, double-click on Components and click on Printing. Now look in the right-hand panel for the name of your printer, and next to it you'll find the driver name, version number and date you need.

System Information is not available in Windows 95 so we suggest you go through the motions of printing and, in the printer driver's control panel, use the Help system for more information. If you can't date your printer driver, replace it anyway. You might end up reinstalling the same version on top of itself, but this won't do any harm.

Other drivers to check

Any device that's non-standard, such as a keyboard with a volume control or a mouse with additional side buttons, will need drivers if the additional features are to work properly. The same goes for plug-in cards that add extra features to a PC, including TV tuners, video capture cards and DVD decoders. Drivers are also required for devices that use USB ports. These include MP3 players, Pocket PCs and virtually every current camera, scanner and printer. With the increasing popularity of USB as a means of connecting peripherals, you're likely to have quite an array of extra drivers to check.

Drivers you can ignore

When you're trawling through Device Manager looking for information about drivers and file versions, you'll come across some devices that don't seem to need drivers at all. Keyboards, hard disks, CD-ROM drives and DVD drives are all in this category. When you look on their driver tabs in Device Manager, it says that no driver files are required or have been loaded.

Most of these devices do use drivers, but not ones you need to update. They rely on standardised drivers built into Windows, and even though there might be an Update Driver button, you don't need to use it unless you want to refresh the original driver because the old one has been deleted, moved or damaged.

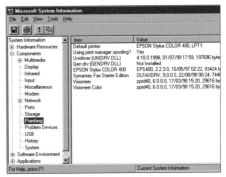

System Information provides in-depth information about drivers for any device, but the amount of detail can be overwhelming. Fortunately, the version number of the Epson Stylus Color 400 printer is easy to find.

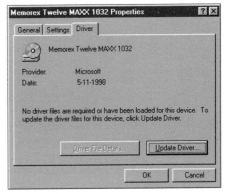

This CD-RW drive, even though it was made in March 2001, is controlled by the 1998 Microsoft driver built into Windows 98. Fitting it involved nothing more than removing the old quad-speed CD-ROM and attaching the new drive to the existing cable.

Once you've compiled a list of the components with drivers that might need updating, and you've jotted down the file versions and dates of the current drivers, it's time to download replacements from the web. To find the sites you need, look in your PC's system manuals for support site locations, or use your favourite search engine and type in the manufacturer's name along with the words 'driver' and 'download'.

1 Once you've arrived at a site, find the driver page (if there's no link to Drivers, try Support or Downloads instead) and compare the latest drivers with the ones on your list. If your existing drivers are out of date, download new ones. When you've clicked to download a driver, you'll be presented with a dialogue box asking you whether you want to run the program from its present location or save it to disk. Always choose to save the program to disk, and make sure you know where it is saved. In fact it's a good idea to make a folder called Driver Updates before you start.

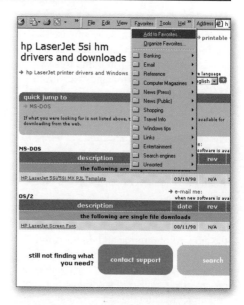

2 Some drivers require you to download several different files so make sure you get them all, and if there are any text files containing installation instructions, get these too. To make things easier, the next time you need to update a driver or tune your PC be sure to jot down web addresses for future reference. Even better, add them to your Favorites by right-clicking on a web page when you visit it and selecting Add to Favorites from the shortcut menu.

3 Not every downloadable file is a driver. Sound cards are usually supplied with utility programs for playing CDs and editing sound recordings. Don't waste time and inflate your phone bill by downloading these if you don't use them. Similarly, graphics card drivers are often coupled with control and utility programs. It may well be possible to install new drivers without updating the controller, though sometimes the two have to be installed as a pair, in which case you'll be warned on the download web page.

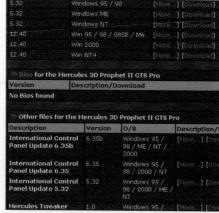

Installing new drivers

Because of the different ways drivers are packaged when you download them (as self-installing programs, as zip files or as bare drivers), installing them can be devilishly simple or fiendishly complicated. In this workshop, we look at how to install all three types of driver package, assuming it has already been downloaded from the web and stored in a folder called Updates.

1 Use Windows Explorer to look inside the folder where you've stored the downloaded drivers. If the file extension is .ZIP, it's a compressed file that you'll have to expand using WinZip or a similar utility. Be sure to place the files in a different folder from the one containing the zip file. Users of Windows Me can treat a Zip file like any other compressed folder and simply double-click it to get at the files within. Having done this, drag the contents into a separate folder (in this case, we've prepared one called Unzipped).

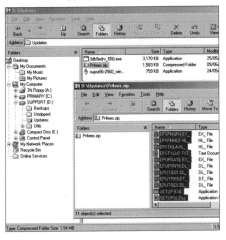

2 If the downloaded driver file has a file extension of .EXE, it's a program you can run by double-clicking it. When you do this, one of two things happens: either the program starts installing the drivers or it merely asks you where to place the files. In the latter case, the program is nothing more than an automated unzipper that performs

the same function as the human operator in step 1. Some manufacturers supply their drivers like this for the convenience of users who don't have an unzipping program of their own.

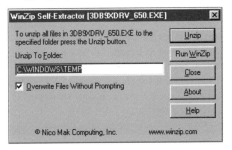

3 If double-clicking a downloaded program file has launched an automated installer, you simply go along with it, responding appropriately to any on-screen instructions. Usually you're not asked anything more taxing than to choose between Full and Custom Installation (always select full unless you know there are features you don't need), and you may be asked to confirm which folder to use. Sound and graphics drivers sometimes demand a reboot after installation; other devices don't, but in our experience it's always a good idea to reboot after installing drivers. We'd also recommend installing one driver at a time with a reboot after each one.

23

 **step by step Installing new drivers**

4 At this stage, either your driver has automatically installed itself or you have some unzipped files in a temporary folder. In the latter case, take a look at the unzipped files and you should be able to work out what to do next. Look first for a file called Readme.TXT. If it's there, double-click it to read it in Notepad. It will tell you how to complete the installation. If there's no Readme.TXT file (or you're in a hurry), look for a program called Setup.EXE or Install.EXE. Either of these is almost certain to be an automated installation program that will respond as described in step 3.

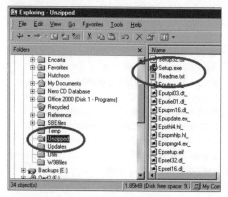

5 If you've got this far without an automated program taking over, it means that the drivers were supplied without a installer and have to be set up manually. These days it's unusual for drivers to be distributed in this way, although Microsoft only describes the manual method under 'Drivers' in Windows Help.

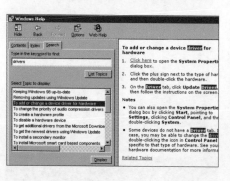

6 We're going to illustrate the process by manually installing a set of drivers for a Diamond Supra 2560 PCI modem. This is a generalised procedure that should work for any set of drivers supplied without an auto installer. The files have been unzipped into a folder called C:\Supra, which contains several .INF files and two readable TXT files.

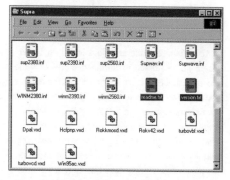

7 Open the System Properties dialogue box (don't forget the shortcut method of Windows key with Pause) and click the Device Manager tab. There are two separate Device Manager entries for modems: HCFMODEM and Modem. This is where Readme.TXT files come in handy. The one supplied with the drivers recommends using HCFMODEM. Double-clicking HCF-MODEM reveals an entry for Supra 2560 PCI Modem Enumerator, and double-clicking this opens its Properties dialogue box. A single click on the Driver tab reveals the current driver, dated 6-24-1999.

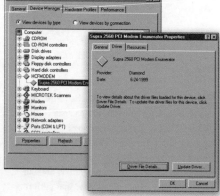

24

Installing new drivers

8 Clicking the Update Driver button starts the Update Device Driver Wizard. Click Next and the Wizard offers two options: to search for a better driver than the one currently in use or to display a list of drivers so you can select the one you want. After selecting the recommended option, which is to search for a better driver, click Next.

9 The Wizard announces where it intends to look for the drivers. Untick all the boxes except the one that says Specify a location, and type the location of the files, which in this example is C:\Supra. If you're not confident about the location of the files, use the Browse button to find them. Click Next.

10 Once the Wizard has located the driver, you'll be prompted to click Next and you'll then see the files being copied from their unzip folder into the Windows system folders. You may be prompted to insert your Windows CD-ROM, so have it ready.

When everything has been copied, the Wizard announces its success. Click the Finish button then the Close buttons on the remaining dialogue boxes.

11 Restart your PC, then return to Device Manager and make sure the modem has been properly recognised. If there is a problem, there will be an exclamation mark next to its entry. A quick look on the Driver tab confirms that the 6-24-99 driver has been updated on 5-28-2001.

After updating the drivers of internal devices, you should find that preferences and settings for the old drivers have been preserved. For a modem, these include transmission speeds and port settings;

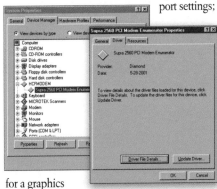

for a graphics card, the resolution and number of colours; and for a sound card, the input and output settings.

Replacement drivers for external accessories such as printers and scanners are less likely to retain their existing settings, so it's worth putting any device whose drivers have been changed through its paces. In the case of a printer, simply do a couple of test prints of recent files, preferably ones including both pictures and text.

25

CHAPTER 3 **Optimising your PC**

What's in this chapter?

With fresh drivers in place, it's time to start tuning your PC in earnest. This chapter covers only the safe tuning techniques built into Windows by Microsoft. They're safe in the sense that they can be reversed easily if they cause any adverse effects. None of them will damage your PC permanently. Don't expect to see massive performance

The message that this PC is configured for optimal performance simply means that you've got enough memory to run Windows, and there are no faults.

gains as you adjust each setting. Tuning is a gradual process, in which small gains in a number of places add up to a worthwhile overall improvement. We don't present you with a prescriptive list of tuning tasks to follow slavishly. Instead, we try to explain what each setting does so you can decide what's best for your machine and your way of working.

Performance settings

The starting point for any tune-up is the Performance section of the System Properties dialogue box. Start System Properties from within Control Panel or right-click My Computer on the Desktop and select Properties. Click the Performance tab and take a look at the summary of your system presented on this sheet.

You'll see total system memory (RAM) with free system resources shown below. Don't confuse the two. The free percentage of system resources has nothing to do with the total amount of system memory (64Mb in this case). The significance of system resources is explained in the workshop on installing and using System Resource Meter on page 38.

File system

File system and Virtual memory should both be described as 32-bit, unless you have an old PC that you have converted from Windows 3.1 to Windows 95 or 98 without updating all the Windows system drivers. If there's a message that you are running in 16-bit or MS-DOS compatibility mode, it's almost certainly related to your hard disk controller. Go to Microsoft's website at www.microsoft.com and search for Q130179, which is an article that offers several possible solutions.

The next two lines tell you whether disk compression is installed (see DriveSpace on page 47) and whether there are any PC cards on the system, which is unlikely unless you have a notebook or laptop PC. The message at the bottom of the sheet – Your system is configured for optimal performance – is misleading. It doesn't mean your PC is a red-hot speed demon; it simply lets you know you've got enough memory to run Windows and that the file system and memory are working in 32-bit mode.

Hard and floppy disks

Click the File System button at the bottom of the Performance sheet to reveal the File System Properties box, which has five tabbed sections. Click the one labelled Hard Disk. There are two settings; one for the typical role of the computer and one for read-ahead optimisation. The role of the computer can be set as Desktop computer, Mobile system or Network server; regardless of what sort of PC you have, if it has a fast hard disk and plenty of RAM set the role to Network server. This speeds things up when running several programs at the same time (multi-tasking).

Make sure the slider controlling read-ahead optimisation is set to Full. This allows the drive to read the maximum amount of data in a single pass. Although this takes longer than reading a smaller

amount of data, the extra data are stored in RAM and time is saved later when the next piece of data is found to be already in memory.

After making these changes, click the Floppy Disk tab at the top of the sheet. There's only one setting and you should remove the tick unless you're using a portable computer with a removable floppy disk drive.

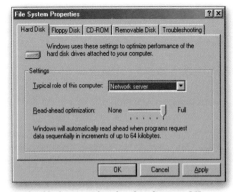

Each tabbed settings sheet has three buttons: OK, Apply and Cancel. The fast way of choosing performance settings is to change a setting then click another tab. This accepts the changes you've made and switches to a different sheet.

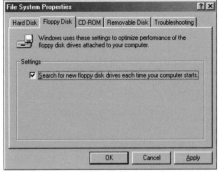

Every time you start Windows, it wastes time scanning for floppy drives. The number of floppy drives in a desktop computer never changes so unless you're using a modular notebook remove the tick. Windows then assumes that the floppy drive situation is the same as the last time it was used.

File system (continued)

CD-ROMs

On the CD-ROM tab (not available in Windows 95) are two settings. The slider controls the size of the supplemental cache, which is a store of memory where the data read from a CD-ROM can be stored for future reference. As with the read-ahead buffer of a hard disk, it can save the PC having to go back for more. It's called a supplemental cache because there is already a cache built into most CD-ROM drives. On a memory-rich system, set the supplementary cache to large, but if you only have 16Mb of RAM set it to small and save yourself a whole megabyte.

The other setting on this sheet is to optimise the access pattern for a particular speed of CD-ROM drive. The top setting is Quad speed or higher, a setting that is now out of date. For many years, every CD-ROM drive has been faster than Quad speed (these days much faster) and if the setting is anything other than Quad speed or higher, change it now. Click on the Removable Disk tab to accept your changes and move on.

Removable drives

Removable drives include 120Mb LS-120 drives (Superdisks), Zip drives, removable hard

disks and various kinds of tape and disk backup drives. The single setting you can change for these (not available in Windows 95) is whether write-behind caching should be enabled.

Write-behind caching means delaying saving data to the removable drive until the computer hasn't got a lot else to do, and the advantage of enabling it is dramatic. Where once there might have been a pause while data were stored on disk, now there is none. Of course the writing of the data will take just as long when it does happen, but if it's at a time when the computer is not burdened with other tasks you won't notice it happening.

By default, write-behind caching is not enabled. This is because there's always a danger that you might eject a removable disk before all the writing has taken place. Provided you bear this in mind, enabling write-behind caching can considerably boost the performance of a removable drive.

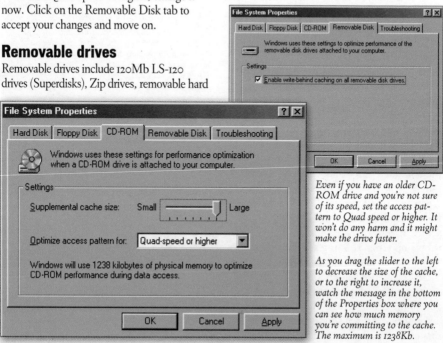

Even if you have an older CD-ROM drive and you're not sure of its speed, set the access pattern to Quad speed or higher. It won't do any harm and it might make the drive faster.

As you drag the slider to the left to decrease the size of the cache, or to the right to increase it, watch the message in the bottom of the Properties box where you can see how much memory you're committing to the cache. The maximum is 1238Kb.

28

Graphics and memory

You can ignore the Troubleshooting tab. There's nothing on this you should change except under expert advice. Most of the settings are concerned with getting Windows to run with older MS-DOS and Windows 3.1 components, and changing these settings without knowing what you are doing is likely to decrease system performance rather than improve it.

Graphics acceleration

Click OK to close the File System section of the Performance tab, then click the Graphics button to view the Advanced Graphics settings. There is one basic option here. The single slider control governs how many of the built-in accelerated features of your graphics card you want to use. The answer, of course, is all of them. In fact the only reason to move the slider to the left and use fewer accelerated features is if the monitor is displaying random errors such as a disappearing cursor, odd blocks of colour or an incompletely drawn screen. Ensure that Full acceleration is selected, then click OK.

Virtual memory

Click the Virtual Memory button and you'll be faced with a performance sheet topped by a prominent yellow triangle containing an exclamation mark. Heed this well because if you choose the wrong settings,

Windows might not start when you reboot. Virtual memory is a strange concept to the uninitiated. It is space on the hard disk pretending to be part of the main system RAM, and although it's there mainly for historical reasons, we're now stuck with it.

When Windows first became popular, memory was vastly more expensive than it is now. Few people could afford to buy a PC with enough real memory to run a graphical operating system like Windows, so Microsoft introduced the swap file, which is an area of hard disk set aside to act as extra memory. A PC with 8Mb of physical memory could use another 8Mb of virtual hard disk memory for a total of 16Mb. Sounds clever, doesn't it? The snag with virtual memory is that hard disks are notoriously slow compared with memory chips, so using virtual memory is like shodding Windows in boots of lead.

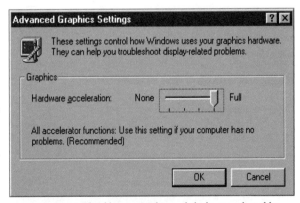

The older your graphics card, the fewer accelerated features it will have and the more likely it is to generate errors with the slider fully to the right. Any card with less than 4Mb of memory is a likely offender.

When you've made changes to any of the system performance settings, you'll be encouraged to reboot your PC. It's OK to say No, but the new settings won't take effect until you do.

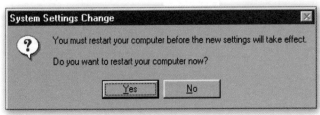

Optimising virtual memory

Use your fastest drive

For the sake of system stability, it's not advisable to disable virtual memory or specify settings different from the ones selected by Windows unless you know what you're doing, but there's a completely safe tweak you can make if you've fitted a new secondary hard disk that is faster than the existing one (as the latest hard disks almost invariably are).

In a normal system, the original drive is designated as C: and the new drive as D:, so by moving the virtual memory from C: to the faster drive D: you can improve overall Windows performance. To do this, select the option 'Let me specify my own virtual memory', then click the arrow to the right of the currently selected hard disk. Choose the new disk from the drop-down list, but don't change any of the other settings. Windows will automatically change the maximum size of the virtual memory to reflect the free space on the new disk. Click OK.

Set your own limits

A more ambitious tweak you can try – but only if you have at least 64Mb of physical RAM – is to specify the minimum and maximum virtual memory settings instead of letting Windows handle them. The advantage of this is that if you specify the same figure for both minimum and maximum memory sizes, the virtual memory file does not shrink and grow as it does when Windows allocates it. It therefore doesn't become fragmented and the hard disk doesn't have to do so much work.

As a guide, for systems with 64–128Mb of physical RAM, set the virtual memory to twice the physical memory. With physical RAM of more than 128Mb, set the virtual memory to 128Mb. Obviously, you wouldn't use this technique on a system that was short of disk space because virtual memory allocated in this way is permanently ear-

marked and never released for other programs.

After working through all the items in the Performance section of the System Properties box, click OK to close it. If you made any changes to any of the settings you'll be prompted to restart Windows, which is essential if you want the changes to take effect immediately.

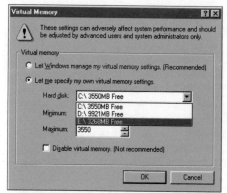

On this PC there are apparently three disks. In reality, C: and D: are two partitions of the same drive, but drive E: is a genuine second disk. Here it is being selected as the new home for virtual memory.

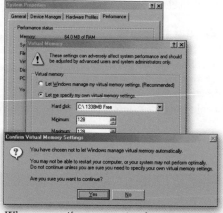

When you specify your own virtual memory settings, as we've done on this Windows Me system, you'll be warned of the dangers. If you run out of memory or find that your system has become unstable, simply switch back to having Windows manage the virtual memory.

30

Desktop and display

In Chapter 5, we take a look at how you can push a graphics card beyond its design expectations, but you can make significant improvements to the reaction time of a graphics card and the quality of the screen image by altering some very straightforward Windows settings. By choosing the right combination of resolution, colour depth and refresh rates, you can make a display less tiring on the eyes, improve the display of colours, and fit more information onto the screen, while by turning off inessential extras such as wallpaper and animations you maximise speed.

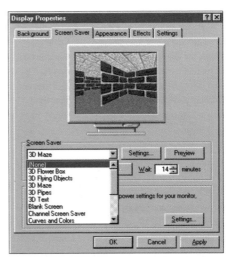

1 Start by right-clicking anywhere on the Windows Desktop, then clicking Properties. Alternatively, double-click the Display icon in Control Panel. The Display Properties box contains five tabbed sheets, and there are performance-enhancing adjustments to be made on all of them. Start by clicking the Background tab.

2 If there is a wallpaper selected, disable it by scrolling to the top of the list of wallpapers and selecting None. The same goes for patterns. Wallpaper and patterns have to be constantly redrawn, which wastes time as well as reducing the total amount of system resources. Of course, if you

get a kick out of pictures or patterns on the Windows Desktop by all means use them. Their impact on performance and resources isn't great, but ditch them if you're looking for maximum responsiveness.

3 Click the Screen Saver tab. Screensavers are even more wasteful than wallpaper in terms of the resources they use, and they can also cause problems by kicking in when they're not wanted, such as

during internet downloads or while trying to make a CD-R recording. Disable them by scrolling to the top of the list of screensavers and selecting None.

4 On the same screen, click the Settings tab to check power management. If yours is a desktop PC, the best setting is not (as you might think) Home/Office Desk, it is Always On. With this selected the hard disk will not spin down and the system will not go into standby. If you want to save the power used by an unattended monitor, select a standby time from the drop-down list next to Turn off monitor. Click OK.

5 Click the Appearance tab. There's nothing you can change here that has a direct impact on performance but you might want to adjust the size of the icons, the icon text, and the spacing of the icon text. If your preferred way of using Windows is with folders and icons on the Desktop, by reducing their size and spacing your can create a bigger work area. Here

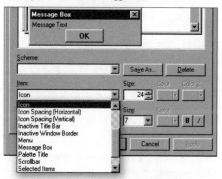

we've reduced icons to 24 points (from 32) and labelled them with 7-point Arial text instead of 8-point MS Sans Serif. This makes an 800x600 screen look like 1024x768. Click Apply after making changes.

6 Click the Effects tab. All the effects slow down your PC. Ideally nothing should be selected, but we like to see Window contents while dragging (instead of just a dotted outline) so we've left this option ticked.

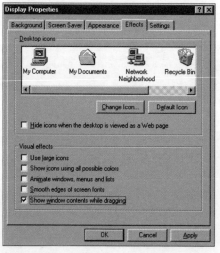

7 Click the Settings tab. On this sheet you can set the desired number of screen colours (known as the colour depth) and the screen area in pixels (known as the resolution). Don't select a 16 colour display: it looks horrible and many programs won't work with anything below 256 colours. The best setting for most graphics cards is 16-bit High Color. Avoid 24-bit colour, which makes a graphics card work as hard as in 32-bit mode but generates fewer colours. When setting the screen area, avoid a resolution of 640x480 unless you have a 14-in monitor that can't manage anything else. 800x600 is good for 15-in monitors and 1024x758 for 17-in. Beyond this it's a matter of personal preference. Click Apply after making your selections.

8 The most important graphics setting (for the sake of your health) is the refresh rate. This is the number of times per second that the screen is redrawn, expressed in Hz. Most people regard 75Hz as flicker-free but others prefer 85Hz. Still in the Display sheet, click the Advanced button, then the Adapter tab. If the Refresh rate panel shows Optimal, it's supposed to be the highest setting your monitor can support. If you can see flicker, select a higher setting in the drop-down list.

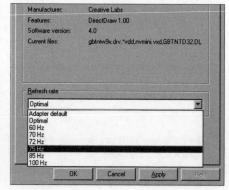

DirectX – the multimedia engine

It's no good setting your graphics card and monitor for optimum performance if Windows isn't capable of generating any high-quality images worth displaying. For this, it needs the latest version of DirectX®, which determines how well a Windows system handles multimedia files of all types.

DirectX was developed in response to programmers (mainly of games) who were rather cheekily bypassing the ordinary Windows channels of communication and making their programs interact directly with graphics cards, sound cards, RAM and other Windows components. The results were impressive but potentially harmful to system stability because Windows couldn't keep track of the resources being used.

DirectX – which includes Direct3D, DirectPlay, DirectDraw, DirectInput and DirectSound – was developed to give programmers the same type of direct access to hardware but without Windows relinquishing control. It has another advantage, which is that it is device independent, so programmers no longer have to write different versions of their programs for different types of hardware. You gain too because if you buy a new graphics card, you know your old programs will continue to work just as well as before.

Checking and upgrading DirectX

DirectX is constantly being developed and improved, and it is vital for a fully tuned PC to have the latest version, which at the time of writing was DirectX 8.1. Compare this with Windows 98, which shipped with DirectX 5, Windows 98 Second Edition with version 6.1, and Windows Me with version 7.1. To find out which version of DirectX you are using, start Explorer, then locate the folder C:\Programs\DirectX\Setup. Here you'll find a shortcut called DxDiag. Double-click this to start the DirectX diagnostic tool, which will tell you which version is

installed. You can find out the latest version of DirectX by visiting the website www.microsoft.com/directx, where you can also download a copy, but because the file size is 11Mb you might prefer to get hold of DirectX from a magazine-cover CD (the most recent version is a standard item on most of them). When you've copied or downloaded the single program file to your hard disk, simply double-click it and a wholly automated upgrade will be performed.

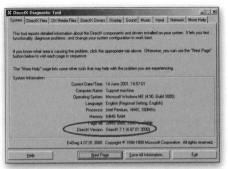

The version number of DirectX can be seen on the System tab of the DirectX diagnostic tool. It's near the bottom, as highlighted here. If you are experiencing problems with graphics, click each of the other tabs in turn and look in the notes section on each sheet for explanatory messages.

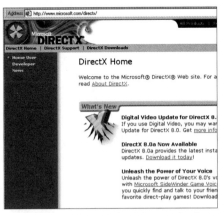

The website at www.microsoft.com/directx is the place to find out about the latest improvements to DirectX. It never does any harm to download and install the version posted here, which is always the most up-to-date.

Disabling background programs

Some programs run parts of themselves automatically whenever you start Windows. This is fine if you really need the facilities they provide, but self-running features are less welcome if they slow down your PC or create conflicts with other programs you frequently use.

One way of stopping programs from running automatically is to remove superfluous entries from the StartUp group. Reach this by clicking the Start button, then Programs, then StartUp. If there's an entry for Microsoft Office, remove it (it's a severe drag on performance). It's safe to remove any other items providing you don't delete them. The best plan is to move them into a spare folder or onto the Desktop until you see whether their removal has made a significant difference. In Windows 98 and Windows Me, you can do this by dragging the entries from the StartUp group to another location. In Windows 95 (where dragging from the Start button is not supported), you have to use Explorer to move the entries, which are initially stored in a subfolder of Windows called Start Menu\Programs\StartUp.

Some auto-running programs bypass the StartUp folder and bind themselves more deeply into Windows by hooking into the Windows Registry. If you're a Windows 98 or Windows Me user, you can disable this type of program using the System Information Utility (in the System Tools folder). Start the program, click the Tools menu, and click System Configuration Utility. You'll see six tabbed sections. Click the right-hand

(Startup) tab to view a list of auto-running programs. Remove the tick from any that you want to disable. You have to restart Windows for the changes to take effect.

Users of any version of Windows can find out what's running by using the Close Program tool, which is invoked by holding down the Control and Alt keys and tapping Delete. In an ideal world, there'd be nothing listed except Explorer, Systray and an anti-virus program, but sometimes it's better to balance convenience against speed and have programs you use frequently running all the time.

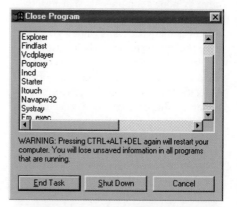

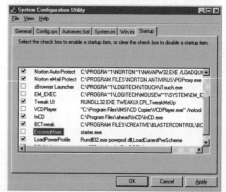

Although you can close a program temporarily using the End Task button in Close Programs, it will be there again after a Windows restart unless you disable it permanently. The best way of doing this is through the System Configuration Utility.

If the tool tray on the right of your Windows task bar looks like the longer of these two, you might be running too many background programs, but don't assume that this is the case. Some icons are there for convenience (the Windows volume control, for example) and don't actually draw on any resources unless you click them.

BIOS tweaks

The BIOS is a chip inside your PC with its own tiny supply of memory where it stores essential information about your system. Changing the contents of this CMOS memory (and thus the BIOS) is not something you'd do in the ordinary course of events, but it can be a boon when tuning. The changes are made using a built-in program that you run outside of Windows. See page 58 for advice on starting and using the CMOS set-up program.

BIOS settings it's safe to tweak

Because every BIOS is different and the settings that suit one PC don't suit another, the best way of finding specific advice on the settings for your PC is to contact the manufacturer or find a user group for your type of PC. The BIOS tweaks on this page are relatively minor (we've erred on the side of safety), but they should work with any type of BIOS.

One way of speeding up the booting of your PC is to enable Quick POST (Power On System Tests) to run fewer tests on the hardware. You can also change the boot sequence so that the BIOS checks the hard disk before the floppy. This stops it grinding away pointlessly searching for a diskette every time you switch on. You can change this setting back at any time if you *do* need to boot from a floppy.

As a general rule, choose to cache the system BIOS and video BIOS but don't cache the video RAM. On the subject of graphics, if you're unlucky enough to have a PC with an integrated display adapter that borrows graphics memory from main memory, use the BIOS to increase the amount allocated to the display to its maximum (usually 4 or 8Mb), but only if you have at least 64Mb of main RAM.

If the first thing you do when you start your PC is turn the Num Lock light off, you might like to save yourself the trouble in

future by setting the Boot NumLock status to Off. Don't tamper with any BIOS settings you don't understand, and do keep a written record of any settings you change, in case you want to change them back.

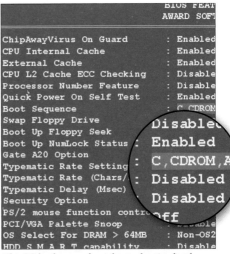

This PC has been configured to try booting first from drive C:, then from the CD-ROM drive and, failing both of these, from a floppy disk. The boot sequence that achieves this is C,CDROM,A.

On page 15 we described how you could 'steal' an interrupt from an unused serial port and give it to another device. Here we see the donor serial port being disabled to prevent any program or accessory trying to use it.

Speedier surfing

Speed and smooth response on the internet depend less on the power of your PC than on the way your modem is set up and the quality of the connection from your internet service provider. There's no escaping the fact that you must have a 56K modem if you're connecting over an ordinary phone line. Don't struggle with anything slower. A new modem will pay for itself in next to no time with lower phone bills – and check with your ISP

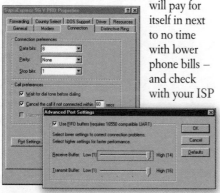

The tick in the box next to FIFO (first in first out) buffers should already be there if you have a 56K modem. Without it, performance will be seriously impaired.

If your hard disk has less than 250Mb free, set a small cache size of 25–50Mb for temporary internet files. Windows can then reclaim the disk space for use as virtual memory. If you have plenty of disk space, go for a big cache.

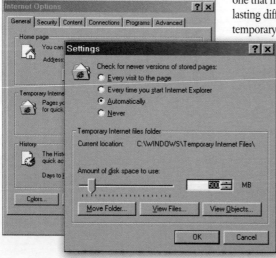

that you're using the best phone number for your type of modem. There may be a FAQ on this topic on your ISP's website.

Modem settings

Adjust your modem for optimum performance by right-clicking My Computer on the Windows Desktop and selecting Properties. In the System Properties dialogue box, click the Device Manager tab. Scroll down and double-click Modem, then double-click the name of your modem. This displays a Properties dialogue box. Click the Modem tab and check that the maximum speed is set to 115,200 bits per second.

Select the Connection tab and click the Port Settings button to reveal two slider controls. The lower slider should already be at its maximum, but the upper one is usually set at 8 instead of 14. Move this slider fully to the right to increase the size of the buffer and accelerate downloading. If you find this causes the connection to be dropped more frequently, simply change it back.

Internet Explorer

Of the many memory caches on your PC, the one that makes the most significant, real and lasting difference to performance is the folder for temporary internet files. This folder stores the contents of the websites you visit, so that when you revisit a site, Internet Explorer draws as much as possible from the cache and you don't have to download everything again. To set the size of the cache, click the Tools menu in Internet Explorer, then click Internet Options. In the General tab, click the Settings button in the Temporary Internet files section. If you have a big hard disk with lots of unused space, set the size of the cache as high as 500Mb. This really makes things fly on the sites you visit regularly.

Speedier surfing (continued)

If you want really fast internet access, you have to pay for it by ditching your modem and subscribing to a broadband service, but this is an expensive option – and one that is still not available in many parts of the UK. The good news is that a 56K modem is really all you need for light to medium internet usage. Provided you regularly get connection speeds of between 38,000 and 45,000 bits per second (you can check this by double-clicking the flashing connection icon on the right of the Windows Taskbar), you should be able to surf comfortably if you remember the following tips.

Making the most of Internet Explorer

The first priority is to make sure you have a secure and relatively bug-free version of Internet Explorer (IE). At the time of writing this means IE5.1 with Service Pack 2 or IE5.5. Version 6 is included with Windows XP and although it will also work with Windows 98 and Windows Me, it's a large download offering few new features . If you're still using IE4 or IE5.0, you should definitely point your browser to www.microsoft.com/windows/ie/downloads/default.asp and get yourself a free upgrade.

With your modem settings tweaked and IE5.1 or higher up and running, try the follow-

ing techniques to speed up your surfing:
● When downloading a file, don't sit around watching the timer. Open a new window and get on with something else. Admittedly the response will be slow but it's better than twiddling your thumbs.
● Open a new browser window with three mouse clicks if you want, but the fast way is Ctrl-N (hold down Control and tap key N).
● On the subject of shortcuts, did you know that the Backspace key takes you to the previous page and Shift-Backspace jumps forward? If you can't remember these, how about Alt-left arrow for backwards and Alt-right arrow for forwards?
● Make good use of the Escape key. You seldom need to read a whole page to find the information you need, so if you've found what you want before a page has finished loading, hit the Escape key and move on.

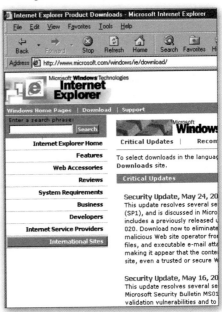

Internet Explorer is frequently updated with patches intended to fix bugs and plug security loopholes, and when there are lots of these and you're not sure which you've already had, it might be easier to completely upgrade Explorer. All your existing settings are retained.

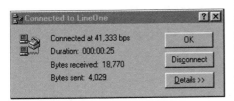

The 56K designation of a modem doesn't mean you can expect to send and receive at 56,000 bits per second. The theoretical maximum receive rate on a perfect line with no other traffic is 56,000bps, but the 41,333bps shown here is quite acceptable. For technical reasons, the maximum send rate on ordinary phone lines is 33,600bps.

The value of System Resource Meter as a tuning aid is not that it makes your PC go faster, but that you can use it to track down programs causing memory errors. The first sign of memory problems is usually a warning message that system resources are low, but in the worst cases you don't know memory is being bled away until you get one of the famous Windows 'bluescreens of death', from which there is no escape other than a reboot.

1 To install Resource Meter, click the Start button, click Settings, and click Control Panel. Double-click the

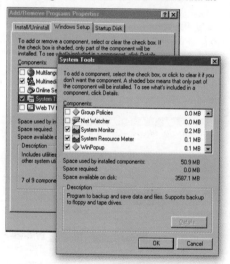

Add/Remove Programs icon to produce a dialogue box, then click the Windows Setup tab. At this stage, Windows 95 users need to select Accessories in the list of components, while Windows 98/Me users should opt for System Tools. Click the Details button, then tick System Resource Meter in the list of components and click OK to continue.

2 Click again on OK to start the installation and be prepared to insert your Windows CD-ROM. If it starts running and

presents you with its opening menu, simply click the X in the top right-hand corner to close it. After the Resource Meter has been installed, you can close Control Panel in the same way.

3 Start Resource Meter from the Start menu by clicking Programs, then Accessories, then System Tools, and finally Resource Meter. This produces a warning from Resource Meter that it might cause your computer to run more slowly. This is true, but the effects are minimal and you won't be running it permanently. Put a tick in the box telling it not to display the message again, then click OK.

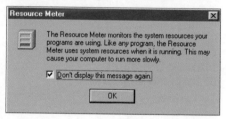

4 The only indication that Resource Meter is running is an icon on the Windows Taskbar. Double-click this icon to view the full-sized Resource Meter, which shows the level of system resources. This is a pool made up of two blocks of memory called the user and GDI (Graphical Device Interface) heaps. Jointly, these contain all the building blocks for the borders, buttons, menus and other familiar objects used by every Windows program. The starting size of this memory is completely unrelated to system RAM in your PC, so it remains the same whether you have 16Mb or 256Mb of main memory.

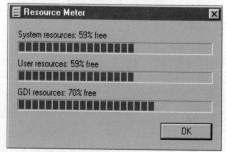

Using System Resource Meter

5 Whenever a Windows program starts, it earmarks a portion of system resources for its private use. When a program closes, it is supposed to return all the borrowed memory to the resource pool, but if a program fails to return the memory – especially when you're running lots of programs at the same time – you might receive a low resources warning, as shown here. When you do, it might already be too late to regain enough memory to continue, but you should try anyway.

6 Rather than wait for a dire warning like the one shown in step 5, you should keep an eye on the Resource Meter icon on the toolbar. When the green bars disappear and you're left with a yellow one, resources are getting low and it's a cue to close any programs you don't need. If you see a red bar, then resources are critically low and you should immediately save all your work, and close down and restart Windows to recover the missing resources.

7 Resource Meter is also invaluable as a means of identifying memory hogs. To use it in this way, double-click the Resource Meter icon on the taskbar and make a note of the three readings (or hover your cursor over the taskbar icon). Start a suspected program, run it for at least five minutes, then exit from it. Give Windows a couple of minutes to settle down, then recheck the Resource Meter settings. You should have

regained all the memory you had before running the suspect program.

8 If you've got a program that hogs resources (there's a blacklist at www.radsoft.net), it's worth visiting the manufacturer's website to see if there's

an updated version. If not, and if it's a program you can't do without, try to run it alone and not when other programs are also making claims on system resources. Another good idea is to avoid closing down and restarting the guilty program because it will steal more memory every time it loads – and always run it with Resource Meter active so you can keep an eye on the taskbar icon for the telltale yellow and red bars.

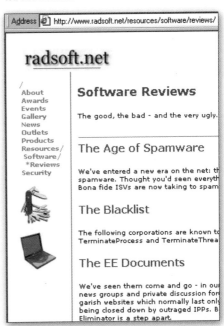

CHAPTER 4 A dynamite hard disk

What's in this chapter?

This might be the most important chapter in this book. What's certain is that the way you tune your hard disk has a significant impact on Windows performance, and nothing else you can do to your PC, short of replacing slow components with faster ones, makes such an dramatic difference.

The reason we didn't deliver this important information earlier is for the good reason that there would be no point in streamlining a hard disk and formatting it for maximum efficiency if you then spoilt it by adding new drivers, deleting old ones and downloading utilities that would reduce the hard disk to a fragmented patchwork of files.

In this chapter, you're going to find out everything you'll ever need to know about disk optimisation and repairs, starting with

the best way of running ScanDisk. The next stage is to reclaim as much space as possible by removing every unnecessary file on your disk – unused programs, unneeded Windows tools, empty folders, temporary files, surplus fonts, and more. What can't be completely removed can be compressed or archived to save space.

Next, we look at setting the most efficient recycling method, and compare the relative merits of using Drive Converter and DriveSpace to increase the capacity of a cramped hard disk. Finally, we use Disk Defragmenter to remove logical gaps on a disk and pack the remaining files into the smallest possible space. The closing workshop covers the advanced technique of partitioning a single hard disk into two or more logical disks.

40

Hard disk health check

Why we don't use Maintenance Wizard

Maintenance Wizard, which is part of the Windows toolkit described in Chapter 8, will automatically run three disk utility programs at regular intervals under the control of Task Scheduler. The three programs are DiskCleanup, ScanDisk and Disk Defragmenter. We don't use Maintenance Wizard for three reasons:

1 A manual disk clear-out is more effective than Disk Cleanup.

2 Using Maintenance Wizard means scheduling tasks for times when you won't be using your PC (which may require leaving it switched on all night).

3 Maintenance Wizard is intended for maintenance only, which is to say that it keeps a tuned disk in tuned condition, but it can't tune a disk for you.

ScanDisk

The first stage in getting your hard disk up to scratch is to check it using ScanDisk. To do this, double-click My Computer on the Windows Desktop, then right-click on Drive C: and select Properties. This will display a pie chart showing you how much of your disk is being used for storage and how much space is left. If you make a note of these settings now you'll be able to recheck them at the end of the chapter and see how much space you've gained.

To run ScanDisk, click on the Tools tab and then on the button labelled Check Now. The fast way to run ScanDisk, which is the best one for regular maintenance, is to select Standard as the type of test and tick the box labelled 'Automatically fix errors'. On this occasion only, and perhaps once a year from now on, you should select Thorough instead of Standard, which does everything in the standard test and then goes on to check every byte of the disk surface for physical errors. This could take

anything from ten minutes to more than an hour, depending on the size and speed of your hard disk.

Click on the Start button to carry out the check. ScanDisk will tell you at the end if it has found and fixed any errors. Use the Close buttons to return to the Windows Desktop.

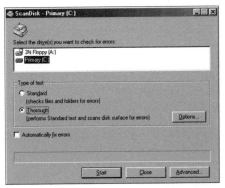

In this example, a thorough scan has been selected but unless a tick is placed in the box next to Automatically fix errors, you'll be bugged with all sorts of questions about how any errors that might be found should be fixed.

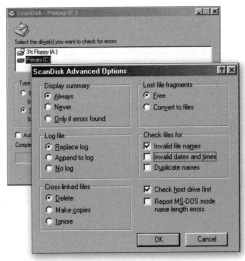

The default options for ScanDisk work fine but we prefer the ones shown here (which leave less clearing up to be done). To use these settings, click the Advanced button, make the selections, then click OK.

Clearing out junk files

Disk Cleanup, which comes with Windows 98 and Windows Me but not Windows 95, identifies and deletes files that are cluttering up a hard disk and that it thinks may be safely deleted. Its main targets are temporary internet files, downloaded program files, offline web pages and the contents of the Recycle bin. To use Disk Cleanup, open the Start menu, point to Programs, point to Accessories, point to System Tools, then click Disk Cleanup.

To be honest, Disk Cleanup is not particularly intelligent. By deleting temporary files, it can actually slow down internet access by forcing you to wait while files you've just deleted are reloaded, yet the space saved will not give any speed boost if there's already plenty of free space on your hard drive. It's better to clean out your hard disk manually, a process that is easy to perform and gives you greater control of what is deleted and what is allowed to remain.

Finding junk files

The definition of a junk file is one that you no longer need on your hard disk. It may once have been very useful (a backup copy of a piece of work or a tutorial video for a program you now know back to front), or it may never have been useful at all. Lots of junk files – weird fonts and clip art you never use – are dumped by programs without your knowledge.

All these and more can be found using the Find feature on the Start button. After clicking Find, select the Files and Folders option and type in what it is you want to look for. Usually this will take the form of an asterisk, a full stop and a three-letter code. For example, *.CHK finds files left behind after ScanDisk has repaired errors and *.TMP finds temporary files. With both these examples, it doesn't matter what's in the first part of a file's name because the asterisk acts as a wildcard. If the three-letter extension matches any file, it will be found.

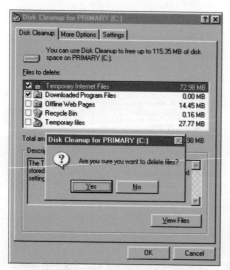

Once Disk Cleanup has identified files to be deleted, it prompts you to click OK. As soon as you do, they're gone forever, whereas if you track down and delete the files yourself, you can recover them from the Recycle Bin or store them in a temporary folder before committing yourself.

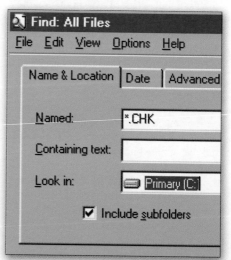

After entering a search term in File Find, be sure to place a tick next to Include subfolders. If you don't, the search will not find every file. Click Find Now to perform the search.

Clearing out junk files (continued)

To speed up the quest for temporary files, you can search for them all at the same time. Just separate the search items with commas. Here's what you'd type if you wanted to look for all the common types of temporary and backup files in a single sweep of the hard disk:

*.TMP, *.SYD, *.OLD, *.BAK, *.CHK, ~*.*, *.~*, *.$$$

Once the files are listed, you can select the ones you want to remove, then click on the File menu and select Delete to remove them (or use the Delete key on the keyboard). The fastest way to get rid of all the files in one go is to hold down Ctrl and press A to select all the files, then use Delete. This method won't work if any of the files are currently in use. You can recognise these because their icons are greyed out in the list of found files. To prevent them holding things up, it's best to clear out junk files after closing all other programs. Even better, do your file finding

before running anything else.

Some other files and folders that it's safe to delete are *.WBK (Microsoft Word backup files), MSCREATE.DIR and ~MSSETUP.T (Microsoft temporary installation files) and README.TXT files. These are documents that tell you about recent changes and amendments to any software you've installed. You don't usually need them once a program is up and running.

Space-wasters

Another way of using the Windows Find feature is look for large files you may no longer need or that you use so infrequently they could be stored on a removable disk. Videos, musical recordings and bitmap photographic images are the main culprits.

One way of identifying them is to search for their file extensions (*.AVI, *.MPG, *.WMV, *.WAV, *.BMP will catch many of the culprits), but to catch them all it's easier to search for bloated file sizes rather than individual file types. Simply click the Advanced tab, leave the file type as All Files and Folders, then look for files of at least 1024Kb to trap everything of a megabyte or more in size.

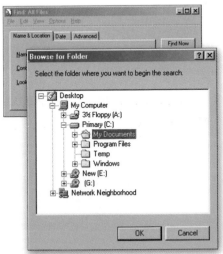

Tip: before searching for bloated files, it's a good idea to restrict the search to the My Documents folder. If you don't, your search will find all manner of programs and supplementary Windows files that you're not really interested in. To limit the search to relevant documents, click the Browse button and navigate to the My Documents folder. Click OK, then click the Advanced tab.

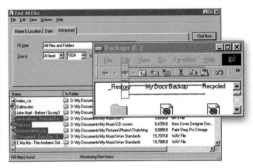

Once all the large files have been found, drag the column boundaries in the Find dialogue box until you can see the Type column. This will give you a good idea of what the file is for and whether it can be deleted safely. Alternatively, drag the files to another disk or folder until you decide what to do with them, as shown here.

Trimming redundant applications

A simple but often neglected way of making space on a hard disk is to delete the programs you never use. You might be surprised at how many of these you can find if you take careful stock. Some may be demonstrations or time-limited samplers from magazine-cover disks; others could be programs you once found useful but that have been superseded by features in newer programs. Take a look at what's on your disk and ditch the stuff you never use. Even if you're not particularly short of disk space, why waste time copying redundant files every time you make a backup?

Don't delete: destroy!

When you delete obsolete programs, it's important to do so using either the uninstaller provided with the program or the Add/Remove programs option in Control Panel. It's definitely not a good idea to man-

ually remove a program by deleting it from the Program Files folder. This leaves stray icons on the desktop and disconnected entries on the Start button menu but, even worse, there could be unresolved entries in the Windows Registry, and these can come back to haunt you in the future.

Even when you remove programs using one of the official uninstall procedures, it's worth using Windows Explorer afterwards to browse the hard disk for folders and files that may have been left behind. The best place to look is in the Program Files folder on drive C:, but it's also a good idea to scan any folders linked directly to the root of drive C:.

If you're not sure which folders can be deleted (their names are usually self-evident), look inside and see if there are any files with an .EXE extension. These are program files whose names might give you a clue. If you double-click them, they might even burst into life, but only if their ancillary files are still intact. Another way of identifying a program is to double-click any file ending in .HLP (these are help files), or look for a README.TXT file that you can open using Windows Notepad.

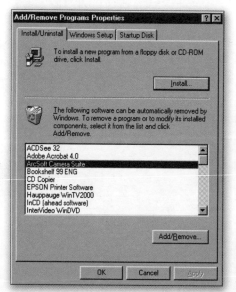

The Install/Uninstall tab in Add/Remove Programs is the recommended way of deleting Windows applications. In this shot, a redundant program is being deleted because its once advanced photo-printing options are now duplicated in other programs.

Many programs come with sophisticated set-up programs that let you install and remove parts of them with ease. Even if you originally went for a full install of a program such as Office 2000, you can retrospectively prune features you find you don't need.

While you're in the mood for ditching excess baggage and you've got Control Panel open, consider removing any Windows modules you don't use. Just click the Windows Setup tab in the Add/Remove Programs dialogue box, then untick the programs you don't need. When you've selected them all, click OK.

Likely candidates for removal are wallpaper, screensavers, document templates, Hyper Terminal, Phone Dialer, Backup (if you've bought something better), sample sounds, desktop themes and multimedia sound schemes. Although you'll probably only be able claw back 20–30Mb by trimming Windows programs, which is nothing compared with what you can save by de-installing a major third-party application, every little counts if you've got an old laptop PC with a non-upgradeable hard disk. Remember: it's not just potential storage you gain – having more disk space means Windows can allocate more virtual memory, and this is particularly useful on older machines with limited physical RAM.

Fling out old fonts

Fonts are a pain. They're often left in place by programs you've uninstalled, and their names and styles can be so similar that the only way to see the differences between them is to view them side by side. Some 'free' fonts are genuinely useful (though in our experience this is rare), while others are a total waste of hard disk space. What's worse, fonts make Windows slower to boot and also increase the loading time of any third-party program that reads the font folder during loading.

There are several ways of deleting fonts, including going through the Fonts icon in Control Panel, but we prefer to use Windows Explorer. Start it up and locate the folder called Fonts, which is in the Windows folder. On the View menu of Explorer, select Large Icons and Hide Variations. TrueType fonts are marked with a blue 'TT' icon and system fonts (which you should never delete) are indicated with a red 'A'.

It's important to set the Hide Variations option because many fonts use families of files, with different ones for bold, italic and other variations. By hiding the variations you can delete all the associated files in one go without having to delete each variation separately.

Removing only the superfluous Windows elements mentioned in the text frees up 26Mb on this Windows 98 PC. This is nothing in terms of a multi-gigabyte hard disk in a new PC but could be invaluable to users of elderly laptops.

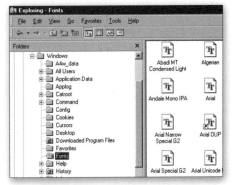

This font folder contains 215 font files taking up 119Mb on disk. None of them were put there by the user. Compare this with 47 fonts occupying a mere 5.5Mb that you find in a fresh installation of Windows 98.

Recycling tour

To see what a font looks like, double-click its icon and a window pops up showing examples of the font in different sizes. Fonts you think you don't need can be removed by right-clicking them and selecting Delete. As with other space-wasting files, if you're not sure whether they're important, you can drag them into a temporary folder and keep them there until you're sure they're not being missed. If you find that a specific font is required by a template or wizard in a design or DTP program, you can drag it back into the Fonts folder.

The Recycle bin

Every Windows user knows that whenever files are deleted they are stored in the Recycle bin until it is emptied. If you've been following these pages 'hands-on', your Recycle bin might now be quite full. When you get around to emptying it, don't neglect to check its size. You can do this at any time by right-clicking the bin and selecting Properties.

If you have more than one hard disk (or if you've split a single drive into two partitions as described in the workshop at the end of

this chapter), you will see a tab for each disk plus one for global settings. If all your disks or partitions are the same size, use global settings. If they're unequal, click the option on the Global tab that says Configure drives independently. Click the tab for Drive C: and move the slider to adjust the allocated storage space. The total size of the drive and the number of megabytes you're reserving are indicated dynamically.

The aim is to reduce the space allocated to the Recycle bin and release disk space for your own purposes or for Windows to use as virtual memory. Even on a massive hard disk with plenty of spare space, it's worth keeping the Recycle bin small to minimise disk fragmentation and keep Windows running faster (see Disk Defragmenter later in this chapter). If you mainly play games and don't create many data files, you probably don't need more than a few megabytes, but if you're into photo-editing you might need 500Mb or more.

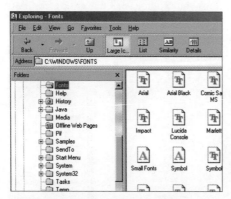

These are the standard fonts in a fresh installation of Windows 98. The TrueType fonts (with variations hidden) are Arial, Arial Black, Comic Sans MS, Courier New, Impact, Lucida Console, Marlett, Symbol, Tahoma, Times New Roman, Verdana, Webdings and Wingdings. Never delete these or any font with a red 'A' icon.

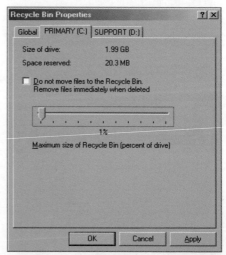

Setting the slider to 1% of this 2Gb drive gives a Recycle bin size of 20.3Mb, which is small but still large enough for light word-processing. If you have two drives and one of them is used only for backups, you can save space by not recycling at all on the second disk.

Drive Converter v. DriveSpace

Drive Converter and DriveSpace are very different in what they do and how they work, but each can be used in its own way to reclaim disk space.

DriveSpace

DriveSpace® evolved at a time when hard disks were very expensive and many PC users were having trouble fitting Windows, a couple of mainstream programs and all their data onto the average 500Mb hard disk.

It used a clever technique of building a single vast file that filled most of a hard disk, then treating this file as a new disk. By applying compression techniques to the file, the virtual disk could be made to hold up to twice as much as its actual size.

You don't get anything for nothing, and the processing power required to compress and decompress all the data going to and from a DriveSpace drive really slows down a PC. Worse still, many disk utilities,

recovery and backup programs don't work well – if at all – on DriveSpace drives. Most of DriveSpace has been dropped from Window Me, but enough of it remains so that Windows Me can recognise and use DriveSpace disks made with earlier versions of Windows.

Drive Converter

Drive Converter is a Windows 98 utility. Like DriveSpace, it can increase the storage capacity of a hard disk, though rather less dramatically. Its real purpose is to convert a hard disk from the old MS-DOS and Windows 95 storage format (FAT16) to the faster and more efficient Windows 98 and Windows Me format (FAT32).

FAT stands for file allocation table, which is an indexing system for hard disk files. A FAT32 index stores information more efficiently than a FAT16 index by splitting files into smaller chunks containing fewer wasted spaces (4Kb instead of 32Kb). By switching to FAT32, you can gain up to 20% more disk space and an increase of several percentage points in overall performance. The negative implications of using FAT32 are few: disk utilities take a lot longer to run and a notebook PC's hibernate-to-disk function might not work, but these drawbacks are easy to live with.

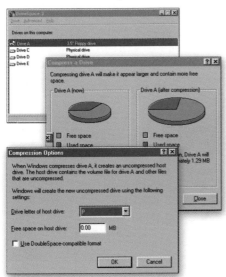

Though DriveSpace can be used to squeeze more onto a floppy disk (the rather complicated procedure shown here promises to increase the free space on this disk from under 1Mb to 1.29Mb), it's really much easier to use a program like WinZip.

If you're not sure whether your hard disk(s) are FAT16 or FAT32, try running Drive Converter anyway. It will tell you if the drives are FAT32 and don't need to be converted.

Drive Converter v. DriveSpace – the winner

There is only one situation where we would really recommend using DriveSpace. It's when you've got a computer that is so old that it's not worth upgrading and you really need to make the most of every kilobyte of its limited hard disk storage space by using the 'on-the-fly' data compression and decompression DriveSpace can provide. In such a situation, increasing storage using DriveSpace might give the machine a few months' extra useful life while you save up for a replacement. This is especially true of older laptop machines equipped with fixed hard disks and no expansion ports capable of accepting an external disk.

Drive Converter is a different matter. If you upgraded to Windows 98 from Windows 95 and didn't convert to FAT32 at the time, you should do it now. Even if you don't need any extra disk space, it will make your PC faster. The only reason not to convert is if you've decided to give DriveSpace a try. You can't use both at the same time because FAT32 and DriveSpace compression are incompatible. This is because DriveSpace works only on FAT16 disks.

Using Drive Converter

Drive Converter is installed by default in Windows 98. Before you convert a disk,

check its properties to see how much free space is on it. There are several ways of doing this, and one that we haven't yet mentioned is from within Windows Explorer. Simply right-click drive C: in the list of Folders to produce the by now familiar Properties box. When you're ready to convert your disk, open the Start menu, point to Programs, point to Accessories, point to System Tools, and click Drive Converter. Follow the on-screen instructions, which seem quite lengthy but involve little more than agreeing with everything you read.

The process involves rebooting your PC and generates some odd-looking on-screen messages, but it takes only a few minutes. You'll then be faced with a much longer wait, possibly hours, while Disk Defragmenter closes up the thousands of gaps that will have been created on the hard disk. If you want to use your PC immediately after converting it, you can click Cancel to halt the defragmentation. If you then recheck the disk's properties, you'll see instantly how much space you've gained, but you won't get the full benefit of FAT32's increased storage until you defragment the disk.

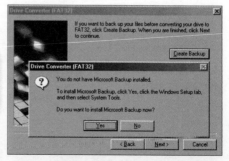

The process of converting a hard disk from FAT16 to FAT32 is almost wholly automatic, but Drive Converter shows you warning messages all the way through. This is not because the process is fraught with danger; it's because it can't be reversed using the tools built into Windows.

Drive Converter invites you to make a backup before it performs the conversion, but then fails to find Windows Backup. We've never heard of FAT32 conversion going wrong, but if you want to be sure we suggest you make your own backup before running Drive Converter.

48

Disk Defragmenter

Fragmentation of a hard disk is caused by the ongoing process of adding, changing and deleting the files stored on it. Gaps left after files have been deleted can be reused, but large files may have to be split into sections to fit in these gaps. They can end up dotted all over the hard disk, which makes retrieving them much slower.

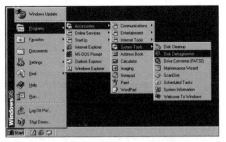

As well as starting Disk Defragmenter in the way described in the text, you'll find it in the System Tools menu along with many of the other tuning tools described in Chapter 8.

The trouble you've gone to updating Windows drivers, optimising Windows settings, converting to FAT32 and trimming the junk off your hard disk in an effort to maximise the space available for virtual memory would all be for nothing without Disk Defragmenter. The disk-based virtual memory would itself become fragmented, and all the performance benefits you had so carefully engineered would be negated. Though

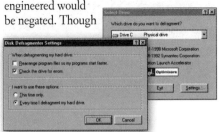

If you interrupt Disk Defragmenter by pressing the Stop button, you'll be presented with the Select Drive dialogue box. Clicking the Settings button leads to a screen where you can untick the box that tells that Disk Defragmenter to rearrange programs to start faster. This greatly speeds up defragmentation.

daily defragmentation is taking things too far (it's a slow process), a weekly session definitely yields performance dividends.

Before running Disk Defragmenter, ditch the contents of the Recycle bin by right-clicking the bin and choosing 'Empty Recycle Bin'. Next, start Disk Defragmenter by double-clicking the My Computer icon on the desktop. Right-click the drive you want to defragment and select Properties. Select the Tools tab and click Defragment Now.

The Windows 95 Disk Defragmenter is faster than those in Windows 98 and Windows Me. This is because the program has evolved over the years not only to close up gaps but also to re-position the most frequently used programs on the most accessible parts of a hard disk. Defragmentation is also much slower on FAT32 disks than on FAT16 disks, simply because there are more 4Kb data clusters to shuffle around than there on FAT16 disks, which use clusters as large as 32Kb.

If you want to see what happens during defragmentation (some people find this unaccountably fascinating), click the two buttons marked Show Details and Legend. The good news is that once you've fully defragged a disk, a regular weekly session shouldn't take much longer than the time it takes to have a coffee break.

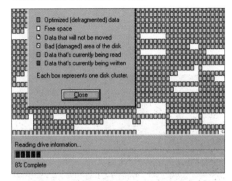

Defragment your disk when no other programs are running. If you don't, it might never finish!

Partitioning a hard drive

When a hard drive is partitioned, it is logically divided into two or more smaller disks. A 10Gb hard disk might be split into two 5Gb disks or into any other combination, such as 7Gb and 3Gb. The reasons for partitioning are various. They include making disk sizes more manageable, being able to put a different operating system on each partition, and the invaluable facility of being able to back up a hard disk onto its second partition without using a removable drive.

1 IMPORTANT! Partitioning a hard disk completely destroys everything that's already on it, and we mean everything – Windows, programs, data, the lot! DO NOT ATTEMPT TO PARTITION YOUR HARD DRIVE UNLESS YOU HAVE A COMPLETE, FULLY TESTED BACKUP AND YOU KNOW HOW TO USE IT. Here we're using Drive Image 5.0, a commercial program, to make an image of this disk before re-partitioning it.

2 You need to make a Windows Startup disk to boot your PC when the hard disk is blank. To make the disk, click the Start button, select Settings, then click Control Panel. When Control Panel opens, double-click on Add/Remove programs.

3 Click the Startup Disk tab. Click Create Disk. You may be asked to insert your Windows CD-ROM and you'll certainly be asked to insert a floppy disk. Click OK when you've done so, then sit back. The rest of the process is automatic.

4 Close down Windows, switch off, then boot with the Windows Startup disk in the floppy drive. You'll soon arrive at this mainly blank screen with a cursor

```
MSCDEX Version 2.25
Copyright (C) Microsoft Corp. 1
     Drive F: = Driver MSCDOC

To get help, type HELP and pres

A:\>FDISK
```

flashing next to an A:\> prompt. From now on, everything you do will be via the keyboard. Type FDISK and press Enter to start.

5 This daunting-looking screen actually asks a single question: "Do you want to use the 32-bit file system?" The answer, for anyone with Windows 98 and a hard disk larger than 2Gb is Y for Yes. Only those with small hard disks that they're planning to compress with DriveSpace should type N for No. Windows 95 users will not be presented with this screen unless they have the later OSR2 edition (as explained on page 11).

```
Your computer has a disk larger than 512 MB. 
includes improved support for large disks, res
use of disk space on large drives, and allowin
formatted as a single drive.

IMPORTANT: If you enable large disk support an
disk, you will not be able to access the new d
systems, including some versions of Windows 95
earlier versions of Windows and MS-DOS. In add
were not designed explicitly for the FAT32 fil
to work with this disk. If you need to access
systems or older disk utilities, do not enable

Do you wish to enable large disk support (Y/N)
```

6 This is the FDISK Options screen. The first thing to do is to delete the existing single partition before making two smaller ones. To do this, choose option 3 (Delete partition or logical DOS drive) and press Enter.

```
Current fixed disk drive: 1

Choose one of the following:

1. Create DOS partition or Logical DOS Drive
2. Set active partition
3. Delete partition or Logical DOS Drive
4. Display partition information
```

7 On the next screen, choose option 1 (Delete Primary DOS Partition) and press Enter. You'll then be faced with a screen like the one shown next, though with different figures for disk space. Here the disk space is reported as 3815Mb even though the current partition is a mere 2047Mb. The reason

Partitioning a hard drive

```
              Delete Primary DOS Partition

Current fixed disk drive: 1

Partition  Status  Type   Volume Label  Mbytes  System  L
  C: 1       A    PRI DOS   PRIMARY      2047    FAT32



Total disk space is  3815 Mbytes (1 Mbyte = 1048576 bytes)



WARNING! Data in the deleted Primary DOS Partition will be lo
What primary partition do you want to delete..? [1]
Enter Volume Label...........................? [PRIMARY
Are you sure (Y/N)...........................? [Y]
```

for this is that prior to FAT32, the maximum size of a Windows partition was 2Gb (2048Mb). Once this disk has been re-partitioned, its missing megabytes will be freed. Press Enter to accept [1] as the partition to be deleted. Type the volume label (this one is called PRIMARY, as can be seen on line four) and press Enter. Confirm with Y for Yes and press Enter.

8 After reading a message that the partition has been deleted, press Esc to continue, which takes you back to the FDISK Options screen. Choose option 1 (Create DOS partition or Logical DOS Drive) and you'll arrive at the screen shown here. Choose option 1 (Create Primary DOS Partition).

```
          Create DOS Partition or Logical DOS Drive

Current fixed disk drive: 1

Choose one of the following:

1. Create Primary DOS Partition
2. Create Extended DOS Partition
3. Create Logical DOS Drive(s) in the Extended DOS Partition
```

9 There's a short wait while the disk is checked and you're then asked whether you'd like to use the

```
Current fixed disk drive: 1




Total disk space is  3815 Mbytes (1 Mbyte = 1048576 bytes)
Maximum space available for partition is  3815 Mbytes (100% )

Enter partition size in Mbytes or percent of disk space (%) to
create a Primary DOS Partition.......................
```

maximum available space for a primary DOS partition. This would result in a single disk of 3815Mb, but when you want to split the disk into two partitions the answer is No. The result is a screen like this one, on which you can change the desired size of the primary partition. We changed 3815Mb to 1500Mb and pressed Enter.

10 A message confirms that the primary partition has been created and you're prompted to press Esc to continue, which takes you back to the FDISK Options screen shown here. The warning message about active partitions can be ignored; the immediate task is to create a second partition by choosing 1 (Create DOS partition or Logical DOS Drive) and pressing Enter.

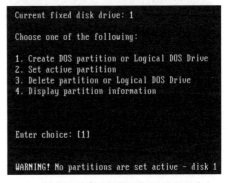

```
Current fixed disk drive: 1

Choose one of the following:

1. Create DOS partition or Logical DOS Drive
2. Set active partition
3. Delete partition or Logical DOS Drive
4. Display partition information


Enter choice: [1]


WARNING! No partitions are set active - disk 1
```

11 This is the same screen as seen in step 8, but with a primary DOS partition already in place the correct choice this time is 2 (Create Extended DOS Partition).

```
                    Create DOS Partition or Logical

Current fixed disk drive: 1

Choose one of the following:

1. Create Primary DOS Partition
2. Create Extended DOS Partition
3. Create Logical DOS Drive(s) in the Extended
```

12 On the next screen we're shown that the total disk space is 3815Mb (no surprises here) and that 1500Mb has already been allocated to drive C:. FDISK does the necessary maths and offers an extended partition of 2315Mb to take up the slack.

This is exactly what we're after so all that's required is a tap on the Enter key to accept the offer.

```
                 Create Extended DOS Partition

Current fixed disk drive: 1

Partition Status  Type    Volume Label  Mbytes   System
    C: 1                  PRI DOS                 1500   UNKNOWN




Total disk space is   3815 Mbytes (1 Mbyte = 1048576 bytes)
Maximum space available for partition is  2315 Mbytes ( 61%
```

13 That's almost it. We now have two partitions, one of 1500Mb and one of 2315Mb. The smaller one is drive C: but the larger one hasn't yet been allocated a drive letter. Press Esc to continue.

```
Current fixed disk drive: 1

Partition Status  Type    Volume Label  Mbytes  System   Usage
    C: 1                  PRI DOS                 1500   UNKNOWN   39%
        2                 EXT DOS                 2315   UNKNOWN   61%
```

14 The message 'No logical drives defined' simply means we haven't yet told FDISK what to do with the 2315Mb extended partition. FDISK sensibly assumes we'd like to use it as a disk drive and offers to create one of 2315Mb. Press Enter to accept the offer (as shown here). On the next screen, which confirms the creation of drive D:, press Esc to continue, which returns you to FDISK Options.

```
No logical drives defined




Total Extended DOS Partition size is  2315 Mbytes (1 Mbyte = 1048576 bytes)
Maximum space available for logical drive is  2315 Mbytes (100% )

Enter logical drive size in Mbytes or percent of disk space (%)...[ 2315]
```

15 There's a warning at the bottom of FDISK Options that no partitions have been set active (the active partition will be home to Windows) so select option 2 to get to the screen shown here. Select 1 as

```
                 Set Active Partition

Current fixed disk drive: 1

Partition Status  Type    Volume Label  Mbytes  System   Usage
    C: 1                  PRI DOS                 1500            39%
        2                 EXT DOS                 2315            61%


Total disk space is  3815 Mbytes (1 Mbyte = 1048576 bytes)

Enter the number of the partition you want to make active.........[ 1]
```

the active partition and press Enter. That's it. Exit from FDISK by following the screen prompts.

16 For the changes to take effect, you must restart your PC with the floppy disk in the drive, after which you can format the primary partition by typing Format C:/S and pressing Enter. When you're warned that all data on drive C: will be lost, press Y for Yes, then Enter (there's not yet anything on this new drive to lose). After formatting, you'll be invited to name the disk. Use your imagination. We typed MAINDISK.

```
WARNING, ALL DATA ON NON-REMOVABLE DISK
DRIVE C: WILL BE LOST!
Proceed with Format (Y/N)?y

Checking existing disk format.
Formatting 1,500.15M
Format complete.
Writing out file allocation table
Complete.
Calculating free space (this may take several minutes)...
Complete.

Volume label (11 characters, ENTER for none)? MAINDISK

1,569,939,456 bytes total disk space
1,569,939,456 bytes available on disk

    4,096 bytes in each allocation unit.
  383,285 allocation units available on disk.

Volume Serial Number is 076D-07F2
```

17 Repeat step 16 for the second disk but use the command Format D: instead of Format C:/S. You now have two logical disks called C: and D:, both formatted but neither containing any data or programs. You can now remove the floppy disk from drive A: and boot in the usual way from the hard disk. Reinstate Windows from a conventional backup, or by using the Restore Image option in Drive Image 5.

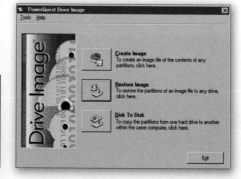

CHAPTER 5 Overclocking

What's in this chapter?

Overclocking means improving a PC's performance by running it faster than its manufacturer intended, so it goes without saying that there are risks – not to you but to the health of your overclocked PC. When you make a CPU run faster, it runs hotter, and the same goes for the processor on a graphics card. If the chips get too hot, they will literally melt internally. The only solution then is to buy a new CPU or graphics card. To give you some ideas of the temperatures involved, most CPUs operate at 25–40°C (it's hot inside a PC) and weak ones start to fail at around 75°C. Few can withstand temperatures over 90°C.

Having got this important warning out of the way, the rest of the chapter leads you through the ins and outs of overclock-ing, and leaves you to make up your own mind as to whether you want to try it. We certainly wouldn't recommend overclocking a CPU unless you have an old, under-powered PC that's surplus to requirements and you're approaching overclocking merely in the spirit of enquiry.

Graphics cards are another matter. Some card manufacturers actually conspire to help you overclock their products by providing tools in graphics drivers that enable you to do it. There's not much point in this if your main use for a PC is to run standard Windows programs, but if your passion is computer gaming and you particularly like 3D action games, overclocking a graphics card, but only at those times when you're actually running games, is an acceptable proposition.

53

Why overclocking is possible

Overclocking originally gained public attention through reports of unscrupulous system builders passing off slow processors as faster ones. We're pleased to say that this practice is now quite rare, mainly thanks to the vigilance of chip vendors. However, it brought public attention to the fact that within a family of processors – Pentium, Pentium III, Celeron, or whatever – the more expensive and faster processors are often identical to the slower ones and have simply been subjected to better quality control and tested for reliability at higher operating speeds.

CPUs and the graphics processors fitted to graphics cards work at frequencies determined by their manufacturers. The frequency of a component, expressed in MHz, indicates how fast it can run. Think of it like a car's rev counter telling you how fast the engine is turning. While it's true that a small engine running at high revs won't necessarily make a car go faster than a big engine running at low revs, when you're comparing two identical cars – or more to the point, two identical PCs – the one running at higher revs will go faster.

Manufacturing tolerances

Overclocking is possible because manufacturers design their products to run reliably at their rated speeds even in the most extreme situations, such as when being used for 24 hours a day inside a PC being used in an overheated, poorly ventilated room and with the system unit crammed with upgrades, add-ons and accessories. Put the same CPU in a well-designed PC with efficient ventilation and a decent cooling fan, and the chances are it will run reliably at a slightly higher speed than its manufacturer's cautious certification, and with aggressive cooling faster still.

Overclocking is therefore the art of speeding up a CPU or graphics card within the margin of safety built into it, but without making it go so fast that it overheats and becomes unreliable. Before attempting to overclock a PC, it's essential to gather information about its current configuration – processor, memory and motherboard.

The best way of cooling an overclocked CPU is with additional fans, but there are software solutions too. AMN Refrigerator is free from www.amn.ru. It works by detecting the short but very frequent periods when a CPU is merely idling and slows it even further to make it run cooler.

The closest thing to a one-stop shop for programs to benchmark, tweak and overclock your PC is www.tweakfiles.com. Everything here is freeware or shareware so the quality is variable.

Overclocking a CPU

The multiplication game

As you might be aware, processors work internally at faster speeds than they are able to communicate with the rest of the PC. This isn't usually a problem. Even though you might think that data would get bottled up in the processor because they can't be sent out fast enough, in practice this doesn't happen. There are several reasons for this, but it's mainly because a CPU seldom has to relay everything it does to another component, and also because ingenious processor designs and the use of high-speed cache memory help to smooth out any imbalances in speed.

The ratio between the internal speed of a CPU and its communication speed is known as its multiplication factor. Two examples will make this clear: a 600MHz Pentium III uses a 100MHz communication bus (bus is the technical term for a data pathway or channel) so its multiplication factor is six. A 594MHz Celeron uses a 66MHz bus so its multiplication factor is nine. If you try to buy a 594MHz Celeron you won't have much luck. Manufacturers and vendors tend to round up speeds to the next 33MHz, 66MHz or hundred MHz, so a 594MHz Celeron would be sold as 600MHz.

Catch the bus for more speed

There are two ways of overclocking a CPU – by increasing the multiplication factor and by increasing the speed of the bus. The first method was once popular (you could turn a 266MHz Celeron into a 333MHz Celeron by increasing the multiplier from four to five), but manufacturers soon cottoned on to this trick and put a stop to it by locking the multiplication factor into the hardware of the processor. Previously it had been determined by switch settings on the motherboard.

Only the owners of what now must be regarded as pensionable PCs – those fitted with Intel 486 processors, classic Pentiums, very early Celerons and anything from the

AMD range of socket 7 processors – can overclock by increasing the multiplication factor. Since the advent of locked CPUs, the preferred method of overclocking is to increase the bus speed.

The **Celeron** has always been a budget version of the Pentium II/III range. As Pentiums get more powerful, so do Celerons, but Intel always keeps them one step behind.

The **Pentium III** is no longer Intel's fastest chip (there's now a Pentium 4) but it's the one that has sold in millions.

The **Athlon** is AMD's rival to the Pentium III, and it delivers equal or superior performance when running at the same clock speed.

The **Duron** is to the Athlon what the Celeron is to the Pentium III.

55

How much can you overclock?

Multiplier

Bus speed	1.5×	2×	2.5×	3×	3.5×	4×	4.5×	5×	5.5×
60	90	120	150	180	210	240	270	300	330
66	99	132	165	198	231	264	297	330	363
75	113	150	188	225	263	300	338	375	413
83	125	166	208	249	291	332	374	415	457
90	135	180	225	270	315	360	405	450	495
100	150	200	250	300	350	400	450	500	550
112	168	224	280	336	392	448	504	560	616
133	200	266	333	399	466	532	599	665	732
150	225	300	375	450	525	600	675	750	825

Bus speed	6×	6.5×	7×	7.5×	8×	8.5×	9×	9.5×
60	360	390	420	450	480	510	540	570
66	396	429	462	495	528	561	594	627
75	450	488	525	563	600	638	675	713
83	498	540	581	623	664	706	747	789
90	540	585	630	675	720	765	810	855
100	600	650	700	750	800	850	900	950
112	672	728	784	840	896	952	1008	1064
133	798	865	931	998	1064	1131	1197	1264
150	900	975	1050	1125	1200	1275	1350	1425

How to use the table

The above table is not exhaustive. It covers processors from the classic Pentium 90 in the top left-hand corner (its 60MHz bus multiplied by 1.5) to most of the recent Celeron, Duron, Athlon and Pentium III processors. You can use the table to view the overclocking options for your processor provided you know the bus speed of your processor and its multiplication factor.

As a rough guide, most Celerons use a 66MHz bus, apart from the 100MHz bus of the latest and fastest Celerons (800MHz and upwards). The Pentium III was designed for a 100MHz bus but it is now also available for a 133MHz bus (which is a bit of a problem because if you have an 800MHz Pentium III you need to know whether it's 8×100MHz or 6×133MHz). Athlon and Duron processors are effectively 100MHz unless they're fitted with special Double Data Rate memory.

To see the overclocking options for a 400MHz Pentium III, which uses a 100MHz bus, look along the 100MHz bus speed line until you get to the 4× column. The official speed of 400MHz is indicated, and if you look one row down you'll see that by increasing the bus speed to 112MHz you will achieve 448MHz. Switching to 133MHz would give you 532MHz, but you'd need to have matching 133MHz memory and very good additional cooling to get away with this sort of increase. As a general rule, only attempt to overclock by moving one row down from your current speed – unless you like living very dangerously.

Preparations for overclocking a CPU

Check memory speed

The CPU overclocking chart on page 56 shows you the next-step-up level of performance you might achieve by increasing the bus speed, but before attempting this you must make sure that your PC's main memory is fast enough to support the new speed. Memory is rated at speeds of 66MHz, 100MHz and 133MHz to match the bus speed of the CPU. Fortunately, most computer manufacturers use faster RAM than they need to, because it increases reliability and performance at very low cost. Many 66MHz Celerons are supported by 100MHz memory, which is easily able to cope with a bus speed of 75MHz. It's not a good idea to overclock a CPU unless the RAM is at least as fast as the bus speed you intend to use.

Keep cool

Take the cover off the system unit and check how the processor is cooled. Even if a fan or fans are already fitted, you'll have to keep speed increments to a minimum unless you introduce supplementary cooling.

● There are software programs such as AMN Refrigerator (free) and Waterfall (commercial) that attempt to keep a processor cool by slowing it down during periods when it isn't doing very much.
● Thermal paste can be applied between the cooling fan and surface of the chip to enhance the fan's cooling effect.
● Additional fans may be fitted to the front or rear panel of a PCs system unit.

● The CPU fan can be replaced with a more efficient model. Cooling clamps fitted with double and triple fans are available. These are sometimes used in conjunction with oversized cooling vanes and ducting systems to channel the air where it's needed most.
● Keep the cover off the system unit during and after overclocking. Only replace it when you're satisfied that your PC is completely stable and not overheating.

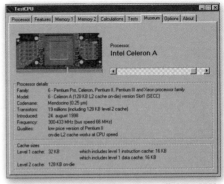

On page 11 we described a free program called TestCPU, downloadable from www.fi.muni.cz/~xsmid4. What we didn't tell you is that as well as identifying the speed and type of your current processor, it contains a museum of information about other processors you might be able to use on your motherboard.

If you don't know the speed of the RAM in your PC, download a tiny utility called DIMM_ID from www.tweakfiles.com. Exciting it's not, but it tells you how many RAM chips there are in your PC, what their capacity is, and how fast they're rated. This PC is using 100MHz (PC100) chips, as indicated on the right of each line.

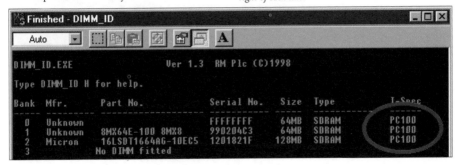

How to change bus speed

We can't tell you how to change the bus speed of your particular PC for the same reason that we can't tell you what make it is – we haven't seen it. However, we can tell you the two main ways in which bus speeds can be set, then it's up to you to read the manual (for the motherboard rather than the PC) to find out which method is appropriate.

Physical switches

On older motherboards that were mainly used for obsolete processors such as the classic Pentium or AMD K6, the multiplication and bus speeds were set by physically manipulating a block of tiny switches on the motherboard or by setting jumpers. A jumper is a push-on connecter that completes a circuit between two copper terminals. Typically, if a jumper is used as a bridge, one speed is set, and if a jumper is removed, a different speed is selected. Sometimes two or more jumpers are used in combination to choose from a range of speeds.

BIOS settings

The more usual way of changing the bus speed these days is through the BIOS. The BIOS is a chip inside your PC with its own tiny supply of memory where it stores essential information about your system. One of these essential pieces of information is the bus speed.

Every PC has a CMOS set-up program that allows changes to be made to the BIOS. Look in your motherboard or PC manual to find out how to invoke this program. You may find it under BIOS Setup or CMOS settings. The technique always involves pressing a particular key or combination of keys during the early stages of the PC boot sequence, and although the Delete key is a favourite there are many other combinations.

Having started the BIOS set-up program, use its menu to go to Chipset Features, where there'll be an option labelled Bus speed, CPU

Host Clock or Clock Speed. To overclock your processor, select the next higher speed, then press Escape to exit the BIOS set-up program. Save your changes before exiting.

This is the Chipset Features section of an Award BIOS. The CPU Host Clock controls the bus speed, which is altered using the Page Up and Page Down keys.

After making changes to BIOS settings, you will be presented with a menu. For the new settings to take effect, you must select Save and Exit Setup. If you're not sure of the validity of the changes you've made, select Exit without Saving.

What's the gain?

If you decide to try overclocking your CPU, please heed our earlier advice and attempt it only on a machine that's surplus to requirements, and limit the increase to one incremental step in bus speed. Trying for a big hike in performance is only possible if you have lots of experience. Those who claim to have made massive speed gains have only done so by spending a fortune on cooling and by tinkering with processor voltages and esoteric BIOS options such as memory timing. We cannot endorse this type of activity.

Testing an overclocked PC

Having overclocked a PC, the first priority is to test its stability and reliability. You do this by running it hard for a couple of hours. Do not leave it unattended because if it shows signs of instability you must be there to switch it off and reset its speed to normal. One way of working a PC hard is to run a succession of benchmarks on it, which will keep the disk, processor and graphics card

busy. Signs to look out for (apart from obvious beeps of complaint and a refusal to boot at all) are blue-screen error messages, unexplained halting of the system, and the picture on the screen breaking up. If you experience any of these, you must reset the bus speed to normal until you have arranged additional cooling. Even with sufficient cooling, not every machine can be overclocked. A single oversensitive chip can lead to instability.

Is it worth it?

Fascinating though it is – and the idea of something for nothing is always a great attraction – overclocking a CPU delivers less than it promises. An increase in processor speed of 10-15% will result in an overall system speed increase of less than 5%. You can make a bigger gain than this simply by defragging a hard disk or switching from FAT16 to FAT32. Keen overclockers will argue that these won't make graphics scroll more smoothly in a multi-player game, and they're right, but if games are your scene then overclocking your graphics card makes more sense than overclocking your CPU.

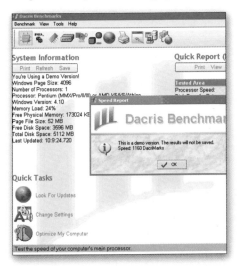

Using Dacris 2001 to test processor speed. The result is given in Dacrimarks. It doesn't matter what a Dacrimark is; what counts is that before increasing the bus speed of this Pentium III machine from 100MHz to 112MHz, the score was 1032 Dacrimarks. Now it's 1160.

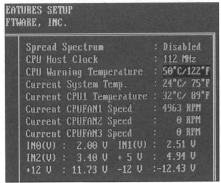

After overclocking and testing a CPU, there's just one thing left to do, which is to go back into the BIOS and set the CPU warning temperature. The maximum safe operating temperature of most CPUs falls between 70°C and 80°C, so set something that gives you plenty of leeway, such as 50°C.

59

Background to overclocking graphics

Overclocking a graphics card is easier than overclocking a CPU, not only because you don't have to open up your PC to make changes, but also because graphics card manufacturers conspire to help you do it. They do this in two ways: sometimes by building 'tweak' controls into the drivers for their graphics cards, but also by producing overclocking tools you can download from their websites.

If the driver for your graphics card lacks a tweak option and you can't find anything for it on the web, this isn't a problem. One of the best overclocking tools for graphics cards can be downloaded as a fully functional demo version from www.entechtaiwan.com. It's called PowerStrip and it enables a high degree of overclocking – far more than graphics card vendors would ever condone – so it needs to be used with care. If you overclock your graphics card too much, you will fry it within seconds. Our step-by-step guide to overclocking your graphics card tells you how to use PowerStrip safely.

One final word of warning. This section on overclocking a graphics card follows hot on the heels of information about overclocking a CPU; this doesn't mean you should tweak them both at the same time.

Overclock one component, then use your PC without glitches for several days before assuming it's safe to overclock the other.

Cooling techniques

Many graphics cards can be tweaked a small amount without additional cooling, but if you want to try for serious performance gains you'll have to find ways of reducing the temperature of the chips on the card. If your graphics card already has a fan, check that it is making good contact with the chip to which it's attached – you could try adding a smear of thermal paste to improve heat transfer. If no fan is fitted (many standard cards simply have a heat sink stuck onto the graphics processor), then fit one. They cost only a few pounds and can be powered by a spare power lead intended for a disk drive. For really serious overclocking, you need a twin-fan card cooler, which clamps over the entire graphics card.

The Blaster Control panel for the Creative Labs TNT graphics card has a Tweak section. Using the slider control you can adjust memory speed from its default of 100MHz to 110MHz, which results in a message warning of the possible effects. To go beyond 110MHz requires a program like PowerStrip.

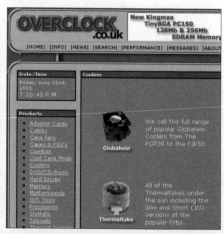

Though you can buy straightforward fans and cooling items from any high-street component shop or computer supermarket, for esoteric cooling options you need to turn to a specialist supplier such as web-based Overclock at www.overclock.co.uk.

Overclocking your graphics card

1 Start by running 2D and 3D benchmark tests to measure current graphics performance. Then obtain PowerStrip from www.entechtaiwan.com. It's smaller than 700Kb and should only take a few minutes to download. Once you've saved the program file onto your hard disk, simply double-click it to install PowerStrip. You'll be presented with screen after screen like this, but you can click Close at any time to start using PowerStrip in earnest.

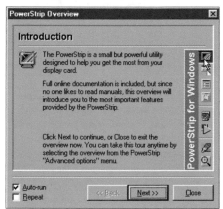

2 PowerStrip places an icon on the right of the Windows Taskbar. Right-click on this and select Show PowerStrip Toolbar. There's no point overclocking the graphics card if it's in a relatively undemanding mode such as 800x600 and 256 colours, so switch to the most demanding combination of

resolution, colours and refresh rate that you're likely to use. You can do this by clicking the left-most icon on the PowerStrip toolbar and making the appropriate selections. Click OK when you've done.

3 The icon of most interest to overclockers is the Information icon on the extreme right of the toolbar. If you click this icon it rather predictably gives you information about the graphics system, but if you *right*-click the icon it leads to the dialogue box shown here, which includes a Performance tab.

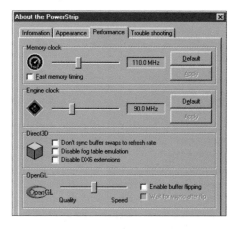

4 There are two slider controls, labelled Memory clock and Engine clock. The engine clock is the processor on the graphics card (which, like your computer's main CPU, can be cautiously speeded up) and the memory clock is the speed of the dedicated memory that supports the graphics processor. This is even more susceptible to upwards adjustment. Start by ticking the Fast memory timing box if it is not already selected.

5 Increase the memory clock before making changes to the engine clock. Start by adding 5MHz and clicking the Apply button. You'll be faced with a warning message that adjusting the clock speed can be dangerous. Click OK to agree.

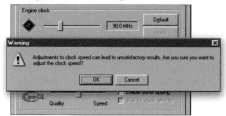

61

6 You now have 8 seconds to confirm that you'd like the change to be implemented. If you fail to click OK during this period, the memory speed drops back to its previous setting. The advantage of this is that if the display has become corrupted because of the changes you've made, recovery is automatic.

7 Continue to increase the memory speed but only in increments of 2MHz. After each increment, study the screen and look for any signs of the picture breaking up. Telltale signs are streaks, stray dots, interference lines or unusual patches of colour. As soon as there are any signs of breaking up (this example is extreme), drop back to the previous speed then subtract another 2MHz to be on the safe side.

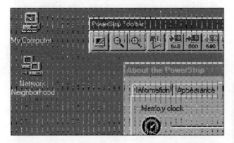

8 In any case, stop if you manage to increase the memory speed by 20%. Here, we've got to 132MHz from a starting point of 110MHz. It might be possible to go beyond this but far better to stop here and run the system for a few days at the new fast settings. Only if no problems arise should you try increasing the memory speed further.

9 Adjusting the engine clock speed doesn't greatly improve performance but it helps to stabilise a graphics card when increases to the memory speed have made the picture break up. The PC in this example starts to exhibit interference when the memory speed

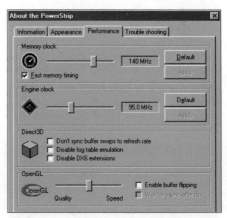

is ramped up to 140MHz, but increasing the engine speed to 95MHz from its starting point of 90 MHz puts things right. To a large extent, the setting of the engine clock is a balancing act. If you increase it slightly, stability improves, but go too far and it deteriorates. Cautious experimentation is the key.

10 Click the Close button to exit PowerStrip's Performance settings, then close PowerStrip itself by clicking the X in its top right-hand corner. Restart your PC before running graphics benchmarks to measure the performance gain.

CHAPTER 6 Keeping in tune

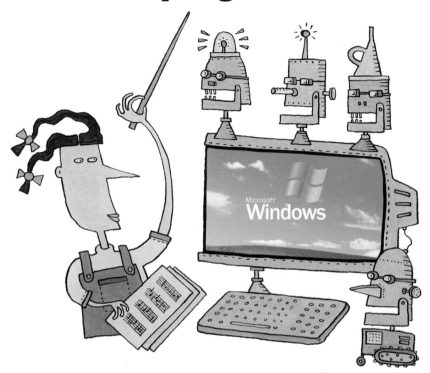

What's in this chapter?

Having done everything you can to get your PC in tune, how do you keep it that way? This chapter looks at the options. You can resign yourself to regular tuning sessions that take up a day or more, or change the way you treat your computer in an attempt to stop it going out of tune.

A new option introduced in Windows Me is a step-back utility that gets you out of trouble by reverting a poorly-working PC to the state it was in the last time it worked properly. You can buy utility programs that do the same thing for Windows 95 and Windows 98. This chapter closes with what we think is the ideal Windows solution, which is to make a full backup of a properly working system and, whenever the PC goes out of tune, reinstate the backup.

Terms of engagement

Keeping Windows in tune is a battle you will inevitably lose, however hard you try. The disk will become fragmented as virtual memory shrinks and grows and as you add and delete files in the normal course of your work. Fragmentation is aggravated by internet usage, because thousands of space-wasting tiny files have to be channelled through a temporary cache whenever you browse the web, and the inbox and outbox of your email program change constantly as messages and attachments are sent and received. Photo editing and graphics programs create massive temporary files, and even relatively innocuous programs such as word processors and spreadsheets create multiple working files for every document that's loaded.

Dealing with dodgy programs

A weekly defrag, as described on page 49, keeps most of the unavoidable fragmentation under control, but what really puts Windows out of sorts is continually installing and uninstalling programs to 'try things out', which is exactly what we're all encouraged to do by computer magazines with CD-ROMs on their covers, and by invitations to download trial programs from commercial websites.

Many of these programs are time-limited; they stop working after a month or so and have to be removed. Some are not even finished (games are often distributed in demo versions before all the bugs have been found) and so-called full programs are nearly always out-of-date versions meant to tempt you into upgrading to the latest release. While this is a great marketing idea, it's one that means up-to-date Windows system files might be replaced by older ones that don't work with your existing software.

It doesn't take many sessions of installing and removing free software to end up with a PC that needs a complete clear-out and tune-up, plus new drivers and perhaps some replacement Windows files.

System Restore

Advocating not installing magazine-cover CDs (or sample programs downloaded from the web) is rather like advocating celibacy as a means of birth control. It works, but it takes a lot of the fun out of life.

Microsoft addresses this problem in Windows Me with a feature called System Restore. This works by recording every change that's made to the files on a hard disk and storing all the data necessary to reverse them. System checkpoints are created automatically when triggered by events (such as installing a new program) and you can add your own restore points at any time. Let's say you load a demo program on Monday evening and then delete it, only to find on Tuesday morning that your PC is no longer working properly. You'd simply instruct System Restore to roll back your hard disk to a restore point prior to the activities of Monday evening.

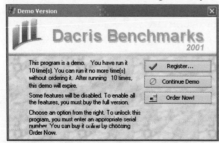

The Dacris 2001 benchmarks are free to try, but after 10 runs they disable themselves. You can uninstall the benchmarks to reclaim disk space, but traces are left behind to prevent you reinstalling the program.

System Restore reserves a minimum of 200Mb of hard disk space for its own use. How far back you can restore from depends on how intensively you use your machine – and on how much extra disk space you're prepared to relinquish.

System Restore v. Microsoft Backup

System Restore sounds great (and within its limitations it works), but there are several reasons why it falls short of expectations as a means of keeping a PC in tune, or as a replacement for a conventional backup regime.

● It can only record around two weeks of disk changes, so the ability to roll back the clock is limited.

● It does not record changes to the My Documents folder or to any files with document extensions such as .DOC or .XLS.

● You can't run System Restore from MS-DOS, so it is of no help when Windows won't start.

● It slows down a PC by involving it in extra disk and processing activity, thus negating many of the advantages of tuning.

If you're a Windows Me user and your PC had at least 200Mb of spare disk space when Windows Me was first installed, then System Restore was activated automatically. The captions for the screenshots on this page tell you how to switch off System Restore (so you can see whether it has been holding back your machine) and how to change the amount of disk space allocated to it.

Microsoft Backup

There is a free Backup program built into Windows. From within Windows, individual files or complete disks may be reinstated, but you can't recover a disk from MS-DOS if Windows won't start. It is this reliance on Windows that limits the program's usefulness. If you want to back up everything on a hard disk, you have to disable every program that may be running (including anti-virus protection) and even then there may be files that do not get backed up because Windows is using them. Another drawback is that if you try to back up onto rewritable CDs, you can't swap discs, and there aren't many hard disks you can squeeze onto a single CD.

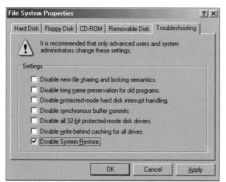

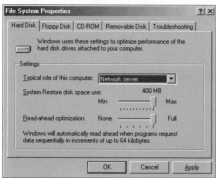

System Restore is configured using options in the File System section of System Properties (see pages 2 7-28). These are not available in Windows 95 and Windows 98. To deactivate System Restore, click the Troubleshooting tab and place a tick in the box next to Disable System Restore. To change the amount of disk space allocated to System Restore, click the Hard Disk tab and use the slider control.

Windows Backup cannot be used from MS-DOS but there is an emergency restore procedure for Windows 98 users only. Start your PC with a Windows Startup disk and then double-click PCrestor.BAT in the tools\sysrec folder of the Windows 98 CD-ROM. This reinstalls enough of Windows to restore your backup.

Drive Imaging

Microsoft's Backup program it is not installed by default in any version of Windows. Users of Windows 95 and Windows 98 may install it using the Add/Remove Programs feature in Control Panel, but things are slightly more awkward for users of Windows Me. They have to navigate to a folder called Add-ons\Msbackup on the Windows Me CD-ROM and locate a program called Msbexp.EXE. Double-clicking this file automatically installs Backup, which then appears, as in earlier versions of Windows, on the System Tools menu. This is accessible by clicking the Start button, followed by Programs, then System Tools.

Drive Imaging

Windows Backup and similar conventional backup programs copy only the files on a disk, but a drive imager works by copying an entire disk partition in one pass as a single enormous file. This image includes not just the files on the original drive but also the information needed to reconstruct the entire partition, including formatting, on a different hard disk. There are two major players in the PC imaging game: PowerQuest (with Drive Image) and Symantec (with Norton Ghost). Both programs confer the same benefits:

● The imaging programs themselves are small enough to be copied to a single floppy disk, which can be made bootable.

● Imaging and restoration can be performed from MS-DOS in order to recover a completely crippled Windows system.

● The creation of images is very fast: typically less than five minutes per gigabyte onto another hard disk.

● If space to store an image is limited, or you want to store it on the minimum number of removable disks, built-in compression can squeeze the image to around half the size of the original.

● If a damaged hard disk has been replaced by a new one, the imaging program is able to recreate the old disk from its image without the user having to partition or format the new disk.

● Supporting programs are supplied for use within Windows to enable users to extract individual files from an image.

● Backups can be stored on multiple CD-RW discs.

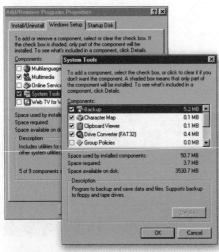

To install Backup in Windows 95 or Windows 98, click the Start button, select Settings, click Control Panel. Double-click Add/Remove Programs, then click the Windows Setup tab. Place a tick next to Backup, which in Windows 98 is in the System Tools group and in Windows 95 is in the Disk Tools group.

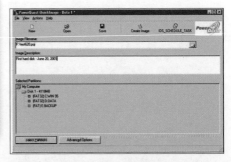

Drive Image presents a Windows-like persona when you run it from MS-DOS, or you can set it up from within Windows and let it perform the DOS operations by itself.

Changing the way you work

Perhaps the most compelling reason for using drive imaging is that the process is so fast and reliable there's no excuse for not using it. If an image is stored on a second hard disk or disk partition, it can restore itself in minutes while you take a short break. This means you can install trial programs with impunity, safe in the knowledge that instead of uninstalling them you can reinstate your fully tuned system from its image.

A new way of working

When backup drives and programs were slow, and the tapes they used were expensive, it would have been insane to propose that ordinary users should keep their PCs in tune by regularly reinstating a complete Windows installation from a backup. Backups were for emergencies only.

Things are different now. Hard drives are amazingly cheap and fitting a second drive to a family PC is a reasonable option. Even without a second drive, hard disks are now so capacious that it's possible to split a standard disk into two or more virtual hard disks using the partitioning techniques described on pages 50-52. An image or backup of the Windows disk can be kept on

the second disk or partition and reinstated quickly whenever required.

Working in this way has only one drawback, which is that if you keep reinstalling an image made in the past you overwrite your recent documents and other important items, such as email messages sent and received, changes to your address book, favourite websites and templates you may have customised. One solution is to back these up separately before reinstating a disk and then restore them afterwards, but this introduces a level of complexity that more or less negates the convenience and speed of the entire system.

It is far better to arrange things so that all the data and ephemeral settings are stored permanently on the support disk; then, when you restore a previous configuration of Windows, it references your current settings and data rather than historical ones. The workshop on the next three pages tells you how.

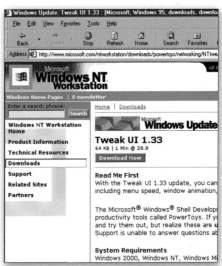

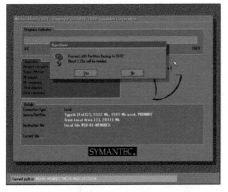

Norton Ghost and Drive Image are extremely robust and reliable. There's little to choose between them in terms of price and performance but Norton Ghost is slightly faster – and easier to use with recordable CD drives.

To help in setting up a dual-disk Windows system, you'll need TweakUI, which can be downloaded from www.microsoft.com/ntworkstation/downloads/ powertoys/networking/NTtweakui.asp. The workshop tells you how to install and use this little gem after downloading it.

This workshop shows you how to spread a standard installation of Windows over two disks. Once you've done this it doesn't matter how often you reinstall drive C: from a backup or image file; it will always run as well as when it was first copied, and it will always reference your latest documents, preferences and settings.

The requirements of the workshop are that you have two physical hard disks, or one hard disk partitioned into two virtual disks according to the instructions on pages 50-52. Drive C: is your usual Windows disk and drive D: is empty. You have downloaded TweakUI as described on page 67.

1 Start Windows Explorer. In the Folders panel on the left, click Drive D: to select it. Click the File menu and, when it opens, select New, then click Folder. A folder called New Folder appears in the right hand pane. Overtype it with the name My Documents and press Enter.

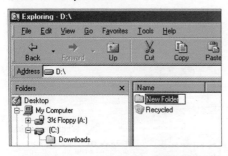

2 Repeat step 1 to create more new folders on drive D: with the names Communications, Favorites, Recent Documents, Send To and Shellnew.

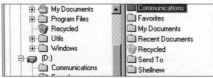

3 Double-click the downloaded TweakUI file to unzip its contents into a temporary folder. In the temporary folder, right-click the file called Tweakui.inf and select Install. An icon for TweakUI will be placed in the Control Panel. Double-click this icon to start the program.

4 In TweakUI, click the My Computer tab. In the drop-down list of special folders, click Document Templates. Click the Change Location button. You'll see a message like the one shown here, warning you of the dangers of changing the locations of special Windows folders. Click Yes to accept the risk.

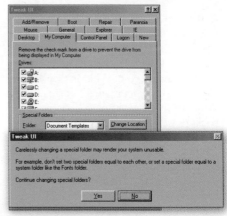

5 A dialogue box with the title Browse for Folder appears. To select a new folder for document templates, scroll down to drive D: and click the plus sign next to it. Select the Shellnew folder you created in step 2 and click OK.

Foolproof Windows recovery

6 Repeat step 5 to change the locations of Favorites to D:\Favorites; My Documents to D:\My Documents; Recent Documents to D:\Recent Documents; Send To to D:\Send To. Click OK when you've finished and you'll be told you need to log off before the new settings take effect. Click OK, but don't log off or restart.

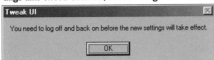

7 Start Internet Explorer. Working offline, click the Tools menu and select Internet Options. Click the Settings button and when the Settings dialogue box appears click the Move Folder button. This produces a Browse for Folder dialogue box identical to the one in TweakUI. Use it to set the location of Temporary Internet Files to (D:). Don't choose a subfolder. Click OK. You'll be prompted to click Yes to restart (as shown here).

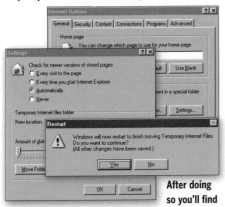

After doing so you'll find that the temporary files have been moved from their old location on drive C: to a new folder called D:\Temporary Internet Files.

8 You'll have to manually transfer the contents of the rest of the old folders – My Documents, Favorites, Recent Documents, Send To and Shellnew – onto drive D:. The easiest way of doing this is to start Windows Explorer twice, then resize the two Explorer windows and place them side by side. Set one copy of Explorer to use drive C: and the other to use drive D:. Drag files from one disk to the other as shown here.

9 Next, change the location of your email folders. If you use Outlook Express, open the Tools menu and click Options. Click the Maintenance tab, then click the Store Folder button. The Store Location dialogue box appears to tell you where the messages are currently stored. Click the Change button and in the Browse for Folder box you can navigate to the folder you prepared in step 2, which is D:\Communications. When you close Outlook Express and restart it, all your email folders will be moved automatically.

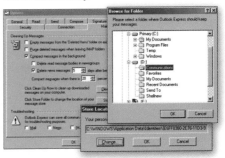

10 If you use the full version of Outlook, as supplied with Microsoft Office, all your email and contacts are conveniently stored together in a single file called Outlook.pst. You should manually move this from its default location of C:\Windows\Local Settings\Application Data\Microsoft\Outlook to D:\Communications. The next time you start Outlook, it will fail to find Outlook.pst, but when you click OK you'll be presented with the dialogue box shown here, through which you can direct Outlook to D:\Communications.

69

11 At this stage, your PC is ready to use. Make a backup or image of drive C: onto drive D: and from this you'll be able to reinstate drive C: whenever it goes out of tune or develops a fault. When you restore the drive, it will continue to reference the up-to-date information you've diverted to drive D:, and as you use the new system you'll think of ways of improving it. Word processor and spreadsheet templates, for example, can be moved to drive D:. Here we see Microsoft Word being told to use an alternative location for its templates.

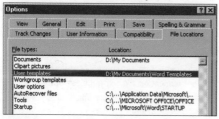

12 It's a good idea to make a folder on drive D: called Utils where you can keep your backup/restore program and any other utilities you think are important. After all, if drive C: won't boot into Windows, it's easier to have the restore program accessible on drive D:

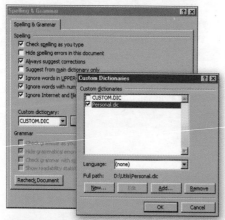

instead of on floppy disks. If you keep a personalised dictionary you should store this with the utilities too.

13 The cookies that store information to identify you and your preferences to the websites you visit are on drive C:, so when you reinstate an image

from D: all the recent cookies you've collected are lost. It is possible (using Regedit) to relocate the cookies folder to D:, but given the potential of cookies to be used by third parties to track your activities on the web we prefer to have them cleansed periodically by the restore process.

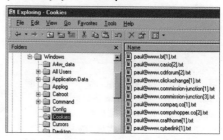

14 Three final tips on using a two-drive Windows configuration effectively:
● Feel free to try out as many new programs, games and golf simulations as you like, but only ever install them permanently after reinstating your backup. Then make a fresh backup.
● If your cookies and newsgroup lists get seriously out of date, spend a session one evening when you reinstall from the backup, then go online and visit all the sites in your Favorites folder and refresh the list of newsgroups. Make a fresh backup immediately afterwards.
● Remember that if drives C: and D: are partitions of the same disk, you're not protected against complete hard disk failure – or the theft of your PC. For total security, as well as the image on drive D: you should still keep a separate backup on removable disks, tape or CDs.

CHAPTER 7 Troubleshooting

What's in this chapter?

It's impossible to tune a PC if it isn't working at all, and it's pointless tuning one that's not working properly. A fast PC that crashes without warning and loses your work is no better than one that grinds along slowly but safely, so this short chapter explains how to identify and fix some common PC problems. The first part tells you how to breathe life into an apparently dead PC, or at least recognise the symptoms of hardware problems that may be preventing it from starting, and the latter part steps you through coping with the problems caused by damaged or missing Windows system files.

Can you fix it?

Replacing missing or damaged files is something you can do yourself, but if you think a hardware repair is needed you'll have to decide whether to do the work yourself or call in a professional. The decision rests on the answers to two questions:

1 Do you have access to a second PC?
2 Is your PC under the protection of a warranty or maintenance contract?

If you have a warranty or maintenance contract, use it. If not, but you can beg or borrow a second PC, it's possible to use it as a donor machine so you can identify faulty components by substitution. Many parts are completely interchangeable between PCs (keyboards, mice, monitors, modems, graphics and sound cards certainly), so it's often possible to identify hardware problems simply by temporarily swapping suspect parts for borrowed ones that are known to be good.

71

When a PC won't even start

Just because a PC won't start doesn't mean it's dead. Here's a step-by-step guide to common problems and quick solutions. These are the sorts of things you'd look for if a machine worked fine when you switched it off yesterday but sullenly refuses to start today.

1 Check that everything is firmly plugged in and turned on, including the switch on the wall socket. It's also worth checking the socket itself (and the mains supply) by plugging in a table lamp. This gives instant visual confirmation that current is flowing. Do make sure that the light itself is working first – try it in a socket in another room.

2 If you know that power is being delivered to your PC but it remains stubbornly inert, doesn't even beep and you can't hear the fan or the hard disk spinning, then it could be that the power supply inside the system unit is defective. This is not a common problem but it does happen. The solution is to have it replaced, but before you haul the system unit off to the repair shop, check its power cable by substituting it for one from another computer appliance. PCs, printers, monitors and scanners all use the same type of cable and it's not unknown for them to suddenly fail after years of

faithful service – especially if they've been tripped over by someone or gnawed by a pet.

3 If there is some evidence of life from the system unit – indicator lights, a spinning hard disk or fan – but no beeping noises and no picture on the screen, the problem may be with the monitor. Check that it is plugged in, turned on and connected to the PC. If there's still no picture (most monitors display a message saying 'No Signal' when they're working OK but haven't been connected to a PC), it could be that the graphics card is defective or has worked loose in its slot. Reseating the card in its slot might help.

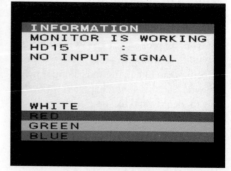

4 Beeping noises from your PC but no picture and no disk activity indicate a faulty circuit board or a loosely connected plug-in component. If you decide to work on the inside of your PC, only do so when it is switched off, but keep the PC earthed by leaving the power cable plugged into the mains socket.

Earth yourself by touching a bare metal part of the PC such as the chassis or power supply. Static electricity can completely destroy PC components so try to avoid touching chips with your fingers, or wear thin rubber gloves if you have them.

5 If you feel brave, take the cover off your PC and locate the motherboard, which is the largest printed circuit board inside a PC and is always screwed to the side or base of the system unit. Check that all the leads, cables and chips connected to it are firmly pushed into their sockets. You can also try removing

any plug-in cards and replacing them in the same slots. Reseating cards in this way often restores a poor electrical connection and if you take your PC to a repair shop this is the first thing they'll try.

6 Beeping noises accompanied by other signs of activity show that the problem is not a dead moth-

erboard. Reseating components as described above might help, but also consider the nature of the beeps. They're not random, and the number and pattern of the beeps indicates the nature of the problem. Of course, this is useful only if you have a manual to tell you what the beeps mean. If you haven't, it's still worth listening to the sequence of beeps so you can describe it to a service engineer or telephone support handler.

Tip!

Sometimes when you reseat a component you suspect has worked loose, Windows rediscovers it as a new piece of hardware. This will certainly be the case if you reseat a component in a different slot. Windows will then ask you to insert its CD-ROM or a disk supplied by the component manufacturer. If the disk isn't readily available and you're sure the required files are already in place on the hard disk, you can use the Skip File button instead. On rebooting, Windows will use the existing files.

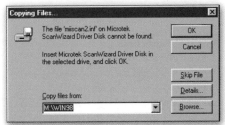

73

Your PC starts, but Windows doesn't

If your PC makes a stab at starting and displays the usual on-screen information about how much memory you have and what the processor is, but then fails to start Windows, look for a descriptive error message. Here are the four most common:

Keyboard error

This can be caused by using the keyboard while the computer is booting, or it may be because a book or other object is resting on the keys. Switching off for a few seconds and restarting a PC sometimes corrects a keyboard error. It's also worth checking that the keyboard is firmly plugged into its socket, and that the mouse and keyboard plugs haven't been switched accidentally. The keyboard nearly always goes in the socket closest to the edge of the case.

If your keyboard and mouse connectors are colour-coded, the plug for the keyboard is lilac and the one for the mouse pale green. Mix them up and your PC won't start.

Floppy disk fail

This usually means the floppy drive's ribbon cable is connected the wrong way round, but this can only happen if you've been working inside your PC and might have had cause to disconnect it. Other causes are

motherboard or floppy drive failure, in which case replacement is necessary, but it may be that the last time you ejected a floppy disk the drive mechanism did not close properly. Try freeing the mechanism by inserting and sharply ejecting a floppy disk a few times before assuming the worst.

Hard disk fail

As with a floppy disk failure, this could be due to the drive being wrongly connected or disconnected. This might happen if you've been working inside your PC on some other problem and may have inadvertently pulled the ribbon cable or power lead from the back of the drive. See step 5 on page 73.

Boot failure

The hard disk may have gone bad or been attacked by a virus, or you may have accidentally deleted some key files from the hard disk. Try booting your PC with a Windows Startup floppy disk and then running ScanDisk by typing SCANDISK and pressing Enter. If files on the hard disk are hopelessly corrupted but the disk is not physically damaged, it may be possible to rescue the data upon it. Seek expert help.

Running ScanDisk from a floppy disk can fix all sorts of hard disk problems, and although ScanDisk can't repair physical damage to the surface of a disk, it can warn Windows to avoid the damaged areas.

Missing or corrupted files

Non-critical errors

The most annoying type of error is one that occurs when your PC is within an ace of starting. Everything seems to be going smoothly and you're expecting the Windows desktop to appear at any moment. Instead you get a black screen containing several lines of text telling you that a file listed for start-up by Windows is missing. The name of the file comes last, followed by an invitation to press any key to continue.

Before you do so you should make a note of the missing file's name. After pressing a key, one of two things happens: either Windows starts despite the missing file or it locks up altogether.

If Windows starts despite the missing file, it could be because the file was not a critical one, or perhaps it was never part of Windows at all but was placed there by a program you have deleted recently. In this case, if reference to the file was not simultaneously deleted from the list in SYSTEM.INI (which Windows refers to when it boots), then Windows might still be looking for it even though it is no longer required. In this case, you can stop Windows looking for the file by unticking reference to in SYSTEM.INI using the System Configuration Utility described in Chapter 8.

Critical errors

If Windows refuses to start because a file is missing, you have a serious problem. By far the easiest solution is to completely restore Windows from a backup – if you're lucky enough to have one. In general, backup programs that allow the reinstatement of individual files can only perform this trick from within Windows, so reinstating the file that is preventing Windows from booting is not an option.

If you're locked out of Windows and don't have a backup, you can always rein-

stall Windows from scratch. This will put things right, of course, but before embarking on such a serious endeavour it's worth checking out the workshop on the next page. It could save you a lot of time.

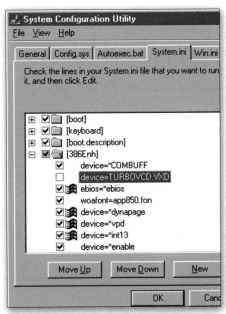

The SYSTEM.INI file may be edited manually in NotePad, but using System Configuration Utility you can enable and disable individual items with greater ease.

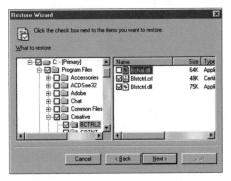

Here are two non-critical files being reinstated using Windows 98 Backup. Because Backup is a Windows program, you can only use it to reinstate non-critical missing files that do not prevent Windows from booting.

Playing it safe

You may have already encountered Windows safe mode and wondered what it was. It kicks in when something serious has gone wrong with the installation of new driver or a new piece of hardware. Safe mode is the minimal Windows configuration. Only those drivers and resources absolutely necessary to start a PC are used.

The default settings are for a VGA monitor running at 640×480 in 16 colours, no network, no CD-ROM drive and a standard mouse. Safe mode doesn't process any of the Windows start-up files or load any superfluous drivers, so it doesn't recognise any accessories – not even internal ones such as a sound card. The plus side is that by ignoring every enhancement, including the one causing the problem, safe mode is nearly always viable when Windows won't load at all in the normal way.

Forcing safe mode

Safe mode is started from the Windows boot menu. If you're a Windows 95 user you invoke the boot menu by powering up your PC and pressing function key F8 when you see the message 'Starting Windows 95'. If you have Windows 98 or Windows Me, all you need do is switch on your PC and hold down one of the Ctrl keys until the boot menu appears. The boot menu is different in all three versions of Windows. There are four options on the Windows Me boot menu, but six in Windows 98 and no fewer than eight in Windows 95.

What can you do in safe mode?

People often scratch their heads over what can be done in safe mode, especially when they can't load anything from CD-ROM and can't run helpful tools like the Add New Hardware wizard. Strange as it may sound, the first thing to try after entering safe mode is to immediately exit and try restarting Windows normally. The very act of invoking safe mode can sometimes be enough to force Windows to correct minor configuration problems. If this doesn't work, you use safe mode to disable the cause of the problem so you can start Windows normally and fix things there.

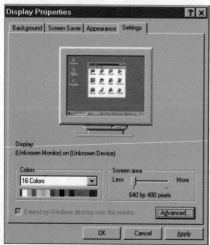

You can't really mistake safe mode. The 16-colour standard VGA display mode is flickery and all the text and icons on the Desktop look improbably large. Just to make sure you get the message, it also says 'Safe mode' in all four corners!

The Add New Hardware wizard is one of many Windows components that won't work in safe mode. Neither will many application programs because they require at least a 256-colour display. Safe mode is really only for problem solving, not for running programs.

Making changes in safe mode

One of the prime causes of a PC booting into safe mode of its own volition is when a new graphics card is installed. The problem is caused by the new graphics card trying to operate with the old card's driver. The solution is straightforward. In safe mode you switch to the standard VGA driver and then reboot before reinstalling the real driver for your new card.

To switch to the standard VGA driver, right-click on the Windows Desktop, then click the Settings tab followed by the Advanced button (called Advanced Properties in Windows 95). On the Adapter tab, click the Change button, then click the Show all devices option. Scroll to the top of the Manufacturers list box and click Standard display types. In the Models panel on the right, click Standard Display Adapter (VGA). Click OK and keep clicking Close until you're told to reboot. All being well, Windows will start normally and you can reinstall the drivers for the new graphics card.

Dodgy devices

Another possibility in safe mode is to disable a hardware device that's preventing Windows from starting normally. The workshop on page 14 describes how you can use Device Manager to activate a device that has been inadvertently disabled. In safe mode, you do the reverse by deliberately disabling a device. This lets you boot Windows normally so you can then go through the motions of reinstalling the device using its driver CD or by physically removing it from its slot and reinserting it so that Windows Plug and Play can take over. You can identify problem devices by the yellow exclamation marks next to their entries in Device Manager. What you can't do in safe mode is interactively resolve interrupt and memory conflicts (because no resources are being used). This is where the resource summary described in Chapter 1

comes into its own. Using this printout you can duplicate settings you know are good and try rebooting. Obviously you won't have any settings for the new (problem) device but you can disable it.

In safe mode the display is always set to 16 colours VGA resolution. What's happening here is not a change of resolution but a change of graphics card driver. All graphics cards should be capable of emulating a standard VGA adapter.

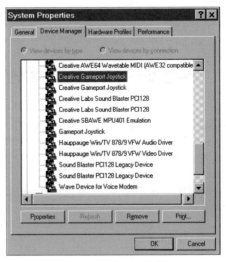

In safe mode it's not unusual to see dual entries in Device Manager. The fact that there are two Creative Gameport joysticks indicates duplicate entry in the Windows Registry, not a genuine conflict. It is safe to remove one of the entries if desired.

Coping with viruses

The old adage about prevention being better than cure could have been coined for computer viruses. Keeping viruses off your machine is dead simple. You install an anti-virus program and then make sure you keep it up to date by regularly logging onto the internet and downloading new virus signatures. Without anti-virus software a virus attack could mean losing the entire contents of your hard disk.

Removing a virus

Anti-virus software should detect an attack before your machine becomes seriously infected. At worst, a single file might be damaged. You'll be asked whether the infected file should be repaired, deleted or quarantined, and usually a repair is the best choice because it involves no reinstatement of lost data or programs.

If the infected file has been damaged beyond repair, you have no choice other than to delete it and replace it with a back-up. Quarantine is no better. It isolates the infected file so it can later be sent to the provider of your anti-virus software for analysis, but it doesn't alter the fact that

you'll have lost the use of the file unless you have a backup.

Some viruses inhabit the boot records of hard disks. Your anti-virus program should be able to remove a boot virus without the loss of data, but it may need the help of an emergency recovery or rescue disk. This is a special bootable disk you are prompted to make when you first install anti-virus software, and from it the boot record of your hard disk can be reconstructed. Neglect to make a recovery disk at your peril.

Serious infection

If a virus finds its way onto your PC because you have no anti-virus software, it will soon spread. Installing anti-virus software retrospectively is worth a try. When you do this, a preliminary scan will be carried out and if a virus is found an attempt will be made to tackle it. However, removing a virus in this fashion is by no means foolproof and, even if it works, a great many files might be lost.

Keeping anti-virus software up to date isn't difficult. Norton AntiVirus warns you when your virus definitions are out of date and offers one-click updates plus links to SARC – the Symantec Antivirus Research Centre.

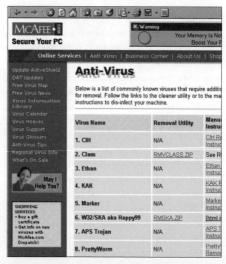

McAfee Anti-Virus is a program with superb web support at www.mcafee.com. There are goodies for the casual visitor too, including a list of ten common viruses with instructions and downloads to remove or neutralise them.

Windows troubleshooters

Microsoft has always recognised that with a complex operating system like Windows, operating on computers cobbled together from hardware and software delivered by thousands of unrelated suppliers, there are bound to be problems. Rather gamely, the company has always included troubleshooters as part of the Windows Help system.

Some people never find the troubleshooters, perhaps because the help systems most of them turn to are the ones built into programs. The main Windows Help system is instigated from the Start button and the assistance it offers is unrelated to the program you are running. In fact, it can be used alongside the Help program.

The troubleshooters have developed along with Windows itself, each version adding more of them, so there are 12 in Windows 95, 16 in Windows 98 and 20 or more in Windows Me. You'll find them on the Help Contents tabs in Windows 95 and Windows 98, and on the Help Home screen in Windows Me, always at the end of the topic lists.

The Windows Me troubleshooters are highly integrated within a browser-like window. Hot links on the right lead to practical solutions.

The TechNet newsgroups now have a Search tool so you don't have to trawl through all the forums to see if anybody has already raised a question similar to yours.

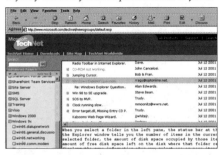

Online troubleshooting

Troubleshooters adopt a step-by-step approach: asking a question, providing a snippet of help, asking if things have changed, providing another suggestion – and so on. Inevitably not every problem can be solved and sometimes the troubleshooter runs out of questions and answers. Windows 95 leaves you to sort things out for yourself, Windows 98 tells you to try Web Help, which directs you to a Microsoft technical support site, and Windows Me provides additional links to a great many MSN® (Microsoft Network) message boards and forums on computing topics.

In fact, similar options are available to you whichever version of Windows you're running. The technical forums are at http://tech.msn.com and the detailed searchable Knowledge Base is at http://search.support.microsoft.com.

There's another useful Microsoft site too, at www.microsoft.com/technet/newsgroups. It is supposed to be a place where 'technical professionals' can swap news and information, but the Windows 9x section is turning into a popular forum where ordinary users can ask questions of other users who may have already solved a similar problem.

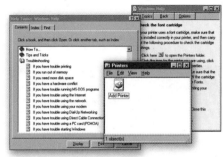

Windows 95 troubleshooters can be confusing if you use several overlapping windows and it's not always easy to retrace your steps to try a different approach.

This workshop steps through the process of repairing a PC that refuses to load Windows because a file is missing or damaged. You can only follow these steps if you have access to another PC running the same version of Windows, which must be Windows 95 or Windows 98.

1 This type of message is disheartening. It tells you a file is missing and it tells you that Windows won't load. You already know this. What it doesn't offer is practical advice about what you can do to put things right. Telling you to uninstall and reinstall the application causing the problem is not really an option when you can't start Windows. The most important thing to do when you see a screen like this is to note down the full location and name of the missing file, exactly as shown. In this case it's:
C:\WINDOWS\SYSTEM\VMM32\IFSMGR.VXD.

```
Cannot find a device file that may be needed to run Windows or a
Windows application.

The Windows registry or SYSTEM.INI file refers to this device file, but
the device file no longer exists.

If you deleted this file on purpose, try uninstalling the associated
application using its uninstall or setup program.

If you still want to use the application associated with this device file,
try reinstalling that application to replace the missing file.

C:\WINDOWS\SYSTEM\VMM32\IFSMGR.VXD
Press a key to continue
```

2 Accepting the invitation to press any key to continue at first produces more screens like the one in step 1, and then the blue screen shown here. 'Your Windows configuration is invalid. Run the Windows Setup program again to correct this problem.' Blue screens are always bad news. They usually signify an unrecoverable error.

```
Invalid VxD dynamic link call from NTKERN(08) + 0000041A to device
"0040", service 0040.
Your Windows configuration is invalid. Run the Windows Setup program
again to correct this problem.

To continue running Windows press Y or ENTER. To quit the current
program press N. If you continue running Windows, your system may
become unstable. Do you want to continue?

    Press Y for Yes or N for No: Y
```

3 However many times you press Y to continue, the file will still be missing. Eventually you'll get the ultimate in bad news, which is a blue screen like this one with a closing message of 'System halted'. At this point you have no alternative but to hit the power switch on your PC. The keyboard and mouse, like everything else, will be dead. There's no way back.

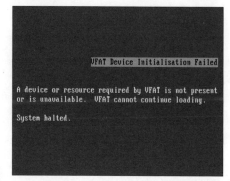

```
                    VFAT Device Initialisation Failed

A device or resource required by VFAT is not present
or is unavailable. VFAT cannot continue loading.

System halted.
```

4 If you're ever going to see this screen again you need three things: the name of the file you copied in step 1, a blank floppy disk and access to a PC running the same version of Windows. You're more likely to be successful if you can match exact versions of Windows (see Understanding Resources on page 11), but if you can't do this you should at least stick to a copy of Windows with the same name as yours: Windows 95 or Windows 98.

Microsoft **Windows 98**

5 Insert the floppy disk into the borrowed PC and start Windows Explorer by clicking the Start button followed by Programs, Accessories, Windows Explorer. Navigate through Explorer until you find the missing file, which will be in the same location as you noted in step 1. In our example, it's a file in the folder C:\WINDOWS\SYSTEM\VMM32, called IFSMGR.VXD.

6 Highlight the file in Windows Explorer and click the right mouse button. On the menu that appears, select Send To and you'll be offered a choice of destinations, one of which is 3.5in Floppy (A). Click this to store a copy of the file on the floppy disk. Don't forget to thank whoever lent you their PC. This is important because you might need it again!

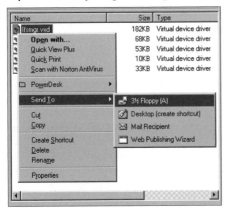

7 Switch on your own PC (don't insert the floppy disk yet) and do whatever is necessary to invoke the boot menu. For Windows 95 this

means pressing F8 when you see the message 'Starting Windows 95...' This works for Windows 98 too but it's hard to hit F8 at exactly the right time so it's easier to hold down one of the Ctrl keys instead. Choose the option 'Command prompt only' and press Enter.

8 Now insert the floppy disk and type:
Copy A:\IFSMGR.VXD C:\WINDOWS\SYSTEM\VMM32
Press Enter.
 Obviously, if you ever have to do this in earnest you'd use the name and location of the real missing file, the pattern being: Copy A:\(insert the filename) C:\(insert the location)
 If you're successful, you'll see the message '1 file(s) copied'. Remove the floppy disk and boot your PC by switching it off for a few seconds then turning it on again.

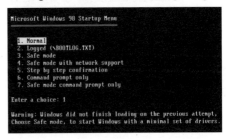

If you get a message that the file is still missing, you've copied it to the wrong location, in which case you should repeat step 8 and make sure you type the location correctly. If you get a new error message about another missing file, you need to repeat the entire procedure to reinstate this file too. They tend to go missing in batches, which is why we said in step 6 you might need to borrow the donor PC again.

CHAPTER 8

The Windows toolkit

What's in this chapter?

When computer buffs talk about software tools they mean programs that have a useful function, not screwdrivers and spanners. In the same way, a software toolkit means a collection of useful programs, not a heavy box full of ironwork.

There's a core toolkit installed by default into Windows. This is in the form of obvious utilities such as ScanDisk, which automatically kicks into action whenever you switch off your PC without closing it down properly, and there are optional tools like System Monitor and System Resource Meter that you have to install yourself. There are even tools tucked away inside other tools, such as the System Configuration Utility hidden inside System Information.

In this chapter, all these utilities are described concisely, with information about whether they are included with your version of Windows, how to locate them and how to start them. We've also indicated whether they are used to diagnose and fix problems or to maintain and tune a healthy system.

Backup

Function: Tuning and maintenance
Description: Microsoft Backup is not a tuning tool, at least not in the sense that it makes your computer run faster, but it is an essential part of PC maintenance. Once you've got your PC running as well as you can, you should make a full backup of the hard disk so that if it goes wrong in the future you can bring it back to its current state of operation by reinstating the backup.
Default or optional component: Optional
Available in: Windows 95, 98, Me
How to start it: Click the Start button. Point to Programs, point to Accessories, point to System Tools, and click on Backup.

Windows toolkit - Disk Cleanup

Control Panel

Function: Tuning and maintenance
Description: As its name suggests, Control Panel is where you make adjustments to Windows. It is not a program, it's a system folder containing other tools. What makes the Control Panel folder special is that it cannot be deleted or renamed; neither can you drag items into the folder or delete them. However, when you add components to your PC and install new programs on the

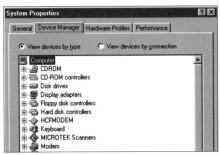

hard disk, you might subsequently find that new tools have been added to Control Panel for you. Even though you can't remove these entries, you can drag them onto the Windows Desktop where shortcuts to them will be created. The shortcuts can then be renamed and given homes on the Start menu so you can get to them more easily.
Default or optional component: Default
Available in: Windows 95, 98, Me
How to start it: Click the Start button. Point to Settings, and click Control Panel.

Device Manager

Function: Fault diagnosis and repair
Description: Device Manager is a mediator between all the different hardware components, or devices, in your PC. It's such an important tool that Chapter 2, in which we demonstrate how to identify Windows drivers and update them if necessary, is completely devoted to it. Device Manager can also resolve conflicts between hardware

components that are fighting with each other over the same resources.
Default or optional component: Default
Available in: Windows 95, 98, Me
How to start it: From the Windows Desktop right-click on My Computer, click Properties, and click the Device Manager tab. You may also start it from Control Panel by double-clicking the System icon, then clicking the Device Manager tab.

Disk Cleanup

Function: Tuning and maintenance
Description: Disk Cleanup identifies and deletes files that are taking up unnecessary space on your hard disk. Legitimate targets include temporary files, downloaded items and the contents of the Recycle Bin.
Default or optional component: Default
Available in: Windows 98, Me
How to start it: Click the Start button. Point to Programs, point to Accessories, point to System Tools, and click Disk Cleanup. A shortcut (but only if the My Computer folder is open on the Windows desktop) is to right-click the drive you want to check, click Properties, then click the Disk Cleanup button.

83

Windows toolkit – Drive Converter

Disk Defragmenter

Function: Tuning and maintenance
Description: Disk Defragmenter has become more refined in the transition from Windows 95 to Windows Me, but its essential purpose remains the same. It removes the gaps that accumulate on a hard disk and

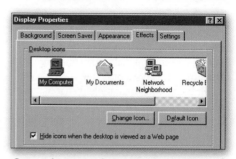

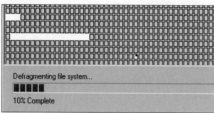

reunites the separated fragments of large files. By doing so, it makes a disk work faster because the read head inside a disk doesn't have to swing madly to and fro searching for the next part of a large file.
Default or optional component: Default
Available in: Windows 95, 98, Me
How to start it: Click the Start button. Point to Programs, point to Accessories, point to System Tools, and click Disk Defragmenter. Alternatively, from the Windows Desktop double-click on My Computer, right-click on the disk you want to check, click Properties, click the Tools tab, and click Defragment Now. The advantage of the first method is that it offers a choice of defragmentation routines, while the advantage of the second, rather long-winded, way of starting Disk Defragmenter is that it tells you how long it is since you last ran it.

Display Properties

Function: Tuning and maintenance
Description: The Display Properties dialogue box is where you can set a number of personal preferences such as backgrounds, colour schemes and screen savers, but it is more important as the starting point for several tuning techniques, including adjusting the resolution, turning special effects on or off and improving picture quality.

Comprehensive information about using Display Properties is on page 31.
Default or optional component: Default
Available in: Windows 95, 98, Me
How to start it: Right-click on a blank area of the Windows desktop, then click Properties. A more convenient alternative if Control Panel is already open is to double-click on Display.

Drive Converter

Function: Tuning and maintenance
Description: The file storage system developed for MS-DOS, called FAT16, was carried over into Windows 95. Windows 98 introduced a different system called FAT32 that wasted less disk space. Drive Converter converts a FAT16 disk to FAT32. The main reason for doing this is to make better use of the available space on a cramped hard disk.
Default or optional component: Default
Available in: Windows 98
How to start it: Click the Start button. Point to Programs, point to Accessories, point to System Tools, then click Drive Converter.

Windows toolkit – Registry Checker

DriveSpace

Function: Tuning and maintenance

Description: In response to user demand, DriveSpace was added to the second (OSR2) release of Windows 95 and carried over into Windows 98. It works by tricking Windows

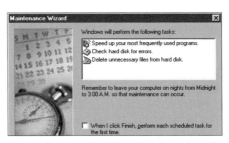

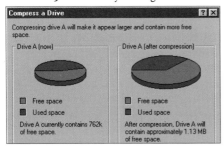

into treating a single large file on a hard or floppy disk as a supplementary virtual disk, and it can almost double the storage capacity of the disk. Unfortunately, there are several reasons why this is not as good as it sounds: DriveSpace disks are slower than ordinary ones, they are more prone to errors, and they are more difficult to sort out if they do go wrong, especially as not all disk repair tools can cope with them. On the other hand, if you've got a notebook PC with a non-removable hard disk that's nearly full, DriveSpace might give it a new lease of life. DriveSpace has been dropped from Windows Me but Windows Me can recognise and read existing DriveSpace disks.

Default or optional component: Default

Available in: Windows 95 (OSR2 only), 98

How to start it: Click the Start button. Point to Programs, point to Accessories, point to System Tools, and click DriveSpace.

Maintenance Wizard

Function: Tuning and maintenance

Description: Maintenance Wizard is a program that sets up three other programs (Disk Defragmenter, Disk Cleanup and ScanDisk) to run under the control of Windows Task Scheduler, though many users prefer to run these programs themselves. The DIY

approach means that Task Scheduler doesn't waste resources by running permanently in the background, and scheduled tasks don't kick in at inconvenient times such as when you're burning a CD-ROM, sending email or downloading files from the internet.

Default or optional component: Default

Available in: Windows 98, Me

How to start it: Click the Start button. Point to Programs, point to Accessories, point to System Tools, and click Maintenance Wizard.

Registry Checker

Function: Fault diagnosis and repair

Description: Though you may not know it, Registry Checker is working for you in the background every time you start Windows. It checks the registry (the central repository of information concerning Windows and the programs installed on it) for errors. If it finds any, it replaces the faulty registry with one of five backup copies it makes automatically. Normally, you don't need to run Registry Checker explicitly, but it can be advantageous to do so at certain times, such as just before making manual changes to the registry.

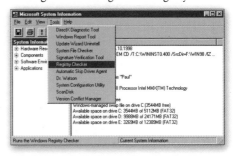

Windows toolkit – System Configuration Utility

Registry checker (continued)

When you run Registry Checker, it lets you make a backup of the current settings, so that if you damage the registry you have a very recent backup to fall back on.
Default or optional component: Default
Available in: Windows 98, Me
How to start it: Click the Start button. Point to Programs, point to Accessories, point to System Tools, then click System Information. On the System Information Tools menu, click Registry Checker.

ScanDisk

Function: Fault diagnosis and repair
Description: ScanDisk is the program that kicks in when you've switched off your PC without closing down Windows properly. This is sometimes unavoidable, such as when your PC has locked up and ceased responding to either the mouse or the keyboard. In this case, crossing

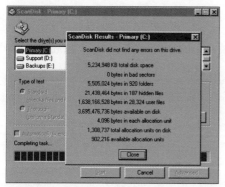

your fingers and hitting the power button is the only option. In its standard mode, ScanDisk finds and fixes most disk problems automatically. There's also an enhanced mode in which it checks the physical integrity of the surface of a hard disk. This is useful when checking out a second-hand PC you're thinking of buying or when the problems ScanDisk has fixed keep recurring for no apparent reason.
Default or optional component: Default
Available in: Windows 95, 98, Me
How to start it: You can run ScanDisk from

Windows, but if Windows won't start and leaves you staring at C:\> prompt on a blank screen, you can start it from there by typing Scandisk and pressing the Enter key. In Windows, click the Start button and point to Programs. Then point to Accessories, point to System Tools, and click ScanDisk.

System Configuration Utility

Function: Fault diagnosis and repair
Description: There are four key text files from which Windows extracts information whenever it starts. They're called AUTOEXEC.BAT, CONFIG.SYS, WIN.INI AND SYSTEM.INI. Information from these files is combined with information from the Windows Registry and the contents of the Windows Startup folder. The System Configuration Utility acts as a one-stop shop where you can make changes to all of these sources of information and enable or disable items individually. By doing this, you can identify Windows problems by trial and error, switching features off until you find the one causing the problem.
Default or optional component: Default
Available in: Windows 98, Me
How to start it: Click the Start button. Point to Programs, point to Accessories, point to System Tools, and click System Information. On the System Information Tools menu, click System Configuration Utility.

Windows toolkit - System Monitor

System File Checker

Function: Fault diagnosis and repair

Description: System File Checker keeps a log of important files kept on your hard disk, particularly those in the Windows folder and some of its subsidiary folders. If you suspect that a file has been changed by a program you've installed, System File

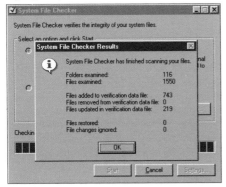

Checker will not only tell you of the change, it will also reinstate the original version of the file. Even more usefully, System File Checker is the easiest way of extracting a single file from a compressed CAB folder. As you will be aware if you've ever searched for an installation file on the Windows CD-ROM, they're not listed individually. Instead they are grouped in more than 70 cabinet files, which can be identified by .CAB at the end of their filenames. Using System File Checker you can view the files within any cabinet and extract them individually. System File Checker is not included with Windows Me but in Windows Me you can extract files from cabinets using Windows Explorer.

Default or optional component: Default

Available in: Windows 98

How to start it: Click the Start button. Point to Programs, point to Accessories, point to System Tools, then click System Information. On the System Information Tools menu, click System File Checker.

System Information

Function: Fault diagnosis and repair

Description: System Information is probably the most useful tool that comes with Windows, but it is often ignored or forgotten. It's not merely a source of information, it's also the launch pad for a number of other system tools, some of which can only be

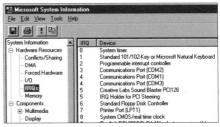

started via the Tools menu of System Information. One of these is the invaluable System Configuration Utility, described on page 86.

Default or optional component: Default

Available in: Windows 98, Me

How to start it: Click the Start button. Point to Programs, point to Accessories, point to System Tools, then click System Information.

System Monitor

Function: Fault diagnosis and repair

Description: A program that runs in the background while you use other programs.

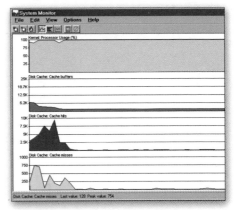

87

Windows toolkit – System Resource Meter

System Monitor (continued)

It displays in pictorial form how hard the disk and processor have to work in different situations. This makes it one of the few tools built into Windows that gives you any indication of whether a tweak or an upgrade to your machine has had any effect.

Default or optional component: Optional
Available in: Windows 95, 98, Me
How to start it: Click the Start button. Point to Programs, point to Accessories, point to System Tools, then click System Monitor.

System Properties

Function: Tuning and maintenance
Description: The System Properties dialogue box is useful as one of the ways of gaining access to Device Manager, but it's also

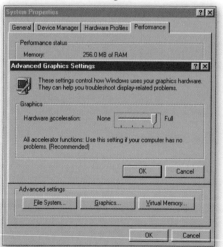

important in its own right as the home of a group of speed-enhancing settings. These are grouped together on the Performance tab. Settings made here affect the perform-ance of hard disks, floppy disks, CD-ROM drives and main memory.

Default or optional component: Default
Available in: Windows 95, 98, Me
How to start it: From the Windows Desktop, right-click on My Computer, and click on

Properties. You may also start it from Control Panel by double-clicking the System icon.

System Resource Meter

Function: Fault diagnosis and repair
Description: You might think that system resources would refer to all the resources a PC can draw on, but it actually means two small 64Kb chunks of memory called the User heap and GDI heap. These are com-bined to form a single pool of system memory that is just one-thousandth of the size of the total 128Mb of RAM found in most new PCs.

You can plug in as much extra memory as you like, but the system resource pool remains the same size. Under normal cir-cumstances, it is sufficient because pro-grams call on the memory only when they need it and release it back into the pool when they've finished with it, but problems arise when you're running too many pro-grams at the same time or when one pro-gram has hogged the memory and won't put it back into the pool. System Resource Meter is the tool that can show you if this is happening. Its installation and operation are described in the workshop on pages 38-39.

Default or optional component: Optional
Available in: Windows 95, 98, Me
How to start it: Click on the Start button. Point to Programs, point to Accessories, point to System Tools, then click on System Resource Meter.

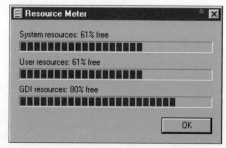

Jargon buster

A AGP Advanced graphics port. Most graphics cards use an AGP-style connector that matches a socket inside the PC. Computers without an AGP socket (because they're old or because they have integrated graphics) are restricted to using slower PCI graphics cards.

B BIOS Basic input/output system. This is an automatic start-up routine that tests your PC and gets it up and running before Windows starts. The BIOS is stored on a chip and is responsible for the strange text messages you see on the screen before Windows starts to load.

Boot To boot (or boot up) a PC is to switch it on and wait for it to start. To reboot is to close it down and then boot it again.

Browser A software program for using the internet. The one built into Windows is called Internet Explorer.

Byte Not quite the smallest unit of storage used by computers, but the one that is easiest to understand. It's enough to store any single alphabetic, symbolic or numeric character.

C Cache An area of memory set aside for storing information so it can be retrieved quickly.

CD-R Compact disc recordable. CD-R blank discs can be recorded once. A special CD-R drive is required to make them but any CD drive can play them.

CD-ROM A special type of CD that can store any kind of data, not just music. It stores 650–700Mb.

CD-RW Compact disc rewritable. Like CD-R but the information on a CD-RW disc can be erased or changed.

Celeron A budget processor made by Intel. Based on the Pentium III but not quite as fast.

Clip art Ready-made images for inserting into your documents.

CMOS memory A special type of memory supported by a small battery so its contents aren't lost when the computer is switched off. The BIOS uses CMOS memory to store important data regarding the clock, drives, set-up and configuration of the PC.

Context menu The menu that appears when you hold down the right mouse button over a selection, option or file. The menu is context-sensitive because it changes according to the task in hand.

Crash Any situation that causes your PC to stop working properly and forces you to restart it.

D Device Any component inside a PC (e.g. graphics card or sound card) or attached to it (e.g. monitor or printer).

Device driver A program (usually small) that acts as an intermediary between Windows and a piece of hardware, passing information between them.

Dialogue box A small window that contains a message and/or options for you to make changes to a program or give instructions to Windows.

DMA Direct memory access. A channel of communication through which a device can cut out the processor and deal directly with memory for added speed.

Document A broad term covering every type of work you can produce with a software program, including spreadsheets, letters, data files, pictures etc.

Driver See Device driver

DTP Desktop publishing. You can do it with nothing more than a word processor, but if the work is to be printed professionally you need a specialised program.

DVD-ROM Digital Versatile

Disc. It stores massive amounts of data on a disk that looks like an ordinary CD-ROM. Used mainly for distributing movies with high-quality video and audio.

E Email Electronic mail is a way of sending and receiving messages using the internet or a closed network such as those used by large companies.

F FAQ Frequently asked questions. A file containing the answers to the questions everybody asks at least once. You'll find them on the internet, especially on manufacturers' support and download pages.

File extension The second part of a file's name, separated from the first part by a dot. It tells Windows (and you, if you're in the know) what the file is for.

Fix A fix is anything that corrects the bugs or errors in a program. It may be a completely rewritten version of the program or a new section to replace the faulty part (see Patch).

Folder A section of a hard disk where you can store related items. Folders can be created and erased as the need arises.

G Gigabyte A measurement of memory so big that it's only used to describe the size of hard disks. 1Gb is a thousand megabytes, which is more than enough to store a bookcase full of information.

Graphics card A card that fits into an expansion slot inside a PC (and can thus be changed). It generates the screen image.

H Hard disk Main storage in a PC for programs and data.

Hz (Hertz) This is a measure of cycles per second, so a 75Hz monitor refreshes itself 75 times per second and a

89

Jargon buster

500MHz CPU ticks at 500 million cycles per second.

I I/O range Input/output range. A range of memory set aside for the exclusive use of a single device in a PC.

IRQ Interrupt request. One of 16 unique codes that a device can use to interrupt the CPU with a request to perform an action. The code identifies the device.

ISP Internet service provider. A company that provides you with access to the internet.

K Kilobyte A measurement of memory capacity but more often used to describe the size of a file or document. One Kb is just over a thousand characters/digits.

M Megabyte A measurement of memory capacity. 1Mb can store roughly a million alphabetic characters, which is as many as in a thick novel.

Memory Something of an overused word in computing, it's any form of storage – including hard drives, disks, CD-ROMs and storage chips. The headline memory figure that you see in PC adverts (usually 32–128Mb) is the capacity of its main memory chips.

Modem A device that converts electronic signals from your PC into sounds that can be sent down a phone line.

Main board See Motherboard

Motherboard The main circuit board inside a PC. It's called the motherboard because all the subsidiary components (CPU, expansion card, memory etc) plug into it.

MP3 A standard means of compressing music so that it requires less storage space but loses hardly any quality.

MS-DOS (DOS) The text-based operating system that everybody used before Windows.

N Newsgroups Discussion groups on the net. You can leave public messages on set topics.

O Operating system This system software (Windows, for example) controls the actions of the different parts of your PC.

P Partition Result of formatting a hard disk in a special way so that it looks like more than one disk.

Patch A replacement section of code that repairs a bug or error in a faulty program. Patches are often provided via the internet because they take less time to download than complete programs.

Pentium A processor made by Intel. The mainstream product is currently the Pentium III. The original Pentium is obsolete, as is the Pentium II (which was functionally identical to the Pentium III). A high-performance Pentium 4 is available.

Peripheral An accessory or add-on, such as a printer or scanner, that plugs into a PC.

Plug and Play Standard devised by Intel to automate the installation and configuration of new computer hardware.

Port A socket or connector on the back of a PC into which accessories can be plugged.

Processor Usually called the 'brain' of a PC, although it's actually just the part that does the computing.

R Reboot See Boot
Refresh rate The image on a computer's screen is constantly redrawn. The refresh rate, expressed in Hertz (Hz), tells you how many times per second.

Registry A central record kept by Windows of the way a PC is configured.

Resolution A measure of the number of dots that make up the picture on a computer screen. The more dots, the sharper the picture, but how many dots you can use depends on the quality of your monitor.

S Search engine A special type of web page where you can type words or phrases and be told on which other internet pages they can be found.

Shortcut An icon providing an easier way of starting a program than finding it on a hard disk. It's a sort of pointer to where a file is stored. Find them on the Windows Desktop and in Windows Explorer.

Sound card An add-on device that plugs into a socket inside a PC to provide its audio output.

T Taskbar Bar running along the bottom of the Windows Desktop, displaying active programs and holding the Start button.

U USB Universal serial bus connectors are a fast and (almost) foolproof means of connecting accessories and peripheral devices to a PC.

W Windows desktop The 'home screen' of Windows. It's what you see when Windows starts, and is home to the taskbar, My Computer and Recycle bin.

Wizard An automated feature in Windows that guides you through a task or activity.

Z Zip drive A high-capacity disk drive. Available in two versions using pocket-sized removable disks capable of storing 100Mb or 250Mb.

Zip file Nothing to do with Zip drives. A Zip file is one that has been compressed to save space and make it cheaper to send over the internet. It has to be expanded to its original size before it can be used.

Index

91

Index